Useful Despair
as Taught to the Hemorrhaging Slave of an Obese Eunuch

Useful Despair
as Taught to the Hemorrhaging Slave of an Obese Eunuch

by Tom Bradley

illustrated by Nick Patterson

MadHat Editions
Cheshire, Massachussetts

MadHat Editions
PO Box 422, Cheshire MA 01225

Text copyright © 2021 Tom Bradley
Illustrations copyright © 2021 Nick Patterson
All rights reserved

ISBN 978-1-7354265-4-9 (paperback)

Cover art and illustrations by Nick Patterson
Book design by MadHat Press and Jonathan Penton

www.madhat-press.com

First Printing
Printed in the United States of America

From the tambourine I have eaten.
From the cymbal I have drunk.
I have borne the cup of gonads.
The room I have entered.
  —Firmicus Maternus

… in the days when mankind was not yet ashamed of its cruelty,
life on earth was more cheerful than it is now.
  —Nietzsche, On the Genealogy of Morals

So are those crispèd snaky golden locks
Which maketh such wanton gambols with the wind
Upon supposèd fairness, often known
To be the dowry of a second head,
The skull that bred them in the sepulcher.
  —The Merchant of Venice III ii 92-6

I.

    Upon the scrotum's fell evacuation
the musculature normally declines—
or so the common wisdom of our time
lets one (that would be me) anticipate.
But here I feel a pair of muscles thrive
on my castrated travel-partner's sides:
handholds for me, lifesaving, living flexures
of human, if not more-than-human steak,
eliciting surprise but no complaint.

    Like most life-residents of our hilled city,
I'm unenthused by water mixed with salt,
especially when sloshed in large amounts.
Just as a blinded Greekling house cat yowls
if bucketed with brine, so do I cringe
from seas, though they be balmy and becalmed
as this, in which we're presently adrift.

    When fishy damp received our shipwrecked party,
I, panicking, dug fists in said companion:
emergency suspension of hands-off,
the policy that governs my behavior
with Spado.

        That's the obese eunuch's name—
and, no, we are not lovers, he and I.
(Pronouns of gender-specificity
are plied advisedly in this account.)

I'm being too dramatic: no "shipwreck,"
to speak precisely, nor so much as "ship."
Our boat, doldrummed, spontaneously split
at seams, or joints—however those are named—
for reasons we mere lubbers of the pavement
can never know.

    Our craft dissolved, I lost
no time deciding we were good as dead,
so reached for Spado by unbrained reflex:
a valedictory grope (you might imply),
expecting hands to gain no firmer purchase
than revelers will find, who un-recline
too quickly at posh banquets, swoon face-first
between Falernian-soused Equestrians,
and on sebaceous flanks of roasted sows
must break their falls.

    But, paradoxically,
beneath the rolls and rolls of gelding pudge
I'm palpating my matched salvation-grips:
thews hard as, with reluctance, I recall
a certain skull to've been, peeled dome of bone
belonging (at least rightfully) to her,
the crone who furnished Spado's new hairdo
eternities ago, when our six soles
still knew the blessed touch of Terra Mater—
at any rate the dreck, between shoe straps,
that winds up wedged in weird Illyria.
(Don't ask why we were there.)

    Her rapèd locks
came loose, unplaited from six crinkly ribands,
magenta-dyed, when, heated honey-like,

our sea-unworthy craft uncrystallized.
Now witchy blondness dangles wetly down
into my eyes and tumbles disarray,
seductively, on drenched cetacean shoulders.

    Exaggerator for effect, that's me:
transsexed rib-woven sinews can't be hard
as barbarous beldams' flint-flayed crania.
But anything that palms remotely firm
seems adamantine when one cannot swim,
and gasps conniptions, liquid to the chin,
solidity unhailed from rim to brim.

    At leisured pace, in nautic gauze, Nemésis
enwrapped us. Spado, gradually, with me
attached, into the watered part of Mundus,
one toe by temperáture-testing toe,
eased us. Soothed bathtime baby-plashy boy,
he blubbed. Such circumstances pose few qualms
for suckling whales.

                For me it's sickly-warm,
as one imagines amniotic sauce
to be, or maybe recollects it as.
Existence dragged beyond the edge of surfeit
this time around, I balk to get re-sucked
into the crumby syrup of the womb.

    The sky is paralyzed, an intimation
of rigor mortis bricked beneath a vault,
with naught by way of meteorology
to euthanize me, nor to kill our boat.
Nevertheless, disintegrate it must,
efficiently as Nero's mother's did

on sly Minerva's recent owlèd Feast,
her last, almost, not quite. No thanks are due
to matricidal offspring's scuttling.

                          Thoughts
of such a glamoured dame summarily dunked
in this identical predicament
inspire our Bathing Beauteousness to mount
operatics of a genre, in all times
and climes affected by the neutered class:

> *I'm blond Agrippina, Imperator's mater.*
> *That pot-bellied Princeps, pale, ginger and snivelly,*
> *abuser of slavelings, dysfunctional satyr,*
> *has fucked me again, this time figuratively.*

  Observing, from beneath disdainful lids,
my seizures, in contralto she intones—

> *Do cleave, if you must, to our sacrosanct person.*
> *This boon you crave's granted by grand Agrippina.*
> *But ride us with dignitas, virile discretion,*
> *you citizen-nursling of Roma Aeterna.*

II.

   I can explain your queen's seaworthiness
no better than our craft's sheer lack thereof,
unless it's *phlégma*'s subtle influence
on surgically induced fluidity.
My handholds notwithstanding, he's a drink
of water.

       Lads from Lebanon I've watched
disporting nude on gentle eastern swells.
They loll like superficial merchant ships,
amphorae tipped in hulls, their ballast slicked
with oil that shuns the flatfish plain beneath.
But Spado's buoyancy's another order.
Not holding at arm's length, Rome's lake maintains
castrati in suspension, ratios
of meat to lymph sufficiëntly low.
He bids extremities to levitate
like anglers' feathered lures, meantime uplifts
his concrete millstone (me) from swallowed death
among pink corals pathics purchase, dredged.

   No treading water for my travel guide.
Testicularly unencumbered, she's
grown nether limbs long as the whole of me,
each dropsied to such admirable degrees
as manageable solely on shinbones
robust as Mémphian obelisks. This bloat,
much like excessive skyward growth itself,
could be unmanning's side-effect.

                              Pliny
the Elder will tell all—if, prior to death,
with throbbing mind and eyes, I ever find
a colonnaded library again.
The latter's mighty research, copied fair,
the scroll-ends smartly pumiced, chamois-wrapped,
might teach me of fluidical retention
induced by dietary indiscretion:
the sumptuous chomping-swilling overdone
by that minority of Spado's peers
indulging selves in something beyond tears.
Meanwhile, physiques, once outraged, reabsorb
diverted semen, transmutating same
to blubber, in a poignant recompense
for—shall we call it "lovelessness"?

                              But who
in my acquaintanceship is less deprived
in that fragrant regard? Vagínal climax
gets demythologized in his context.
Of this I'm too aware while fending swells
and barnacling this member-in-good-stance
of Rome's "third sex," as it's been called.

                              One thinks
a fourth and, on feast days, at least a fifth,
should be accrued, accommodating Spado.

III.

"Ah me!" moos your bosomy old Empress Mother,
her long-suffering, put-upon orbs bluely wincing.
She lows in her horror! Her soft saffron coiffure
might fail to survive such an émphatic rinsing!

   Placental broth is shaken from that halo.
To Illyrian roots bedrenched, it yet retains
exquisite highlights, tinted no less bright
than shimmered on that misremembered night
when scalp from conjure woman's calvaria
was teased, scraped, stretched, perfunctorily tanned.

   Through purloined curls, one sardine skeleton,
love-tribute of a sad, enamored porpoise,
serves Spado for a comb. Just as barrettes,
once creamy-textured tusks coaxed solemnly
from worshipped Indus elephants' god-gums,
are fine-tooth carved, then fetched into our bourne,
transshipped at sultry Felix Araby
by Erythréan mates, monsoon-shampooed,
with cinnamony epidermises,
ungrammared tongues, exotic appetites
and pendulously black—

               Apologies
for that curtailed Homeric simile.
It oozed up from a rank, blind foetal bowel.
Please rest assured your narrator will hew
to Stoic principles, while reverencing,
through stern anachronistical comportment,

our fathers' late Republic—rather, mine,
for who can tell whence óbese eunuchs whelp?

   For example, I'll remain incapable,
by temperament reluctant as a vestal,
to guess if fingers, unintentioned, ten,
are tickling unsexed axillae. Cling tight
or drown's the watchword, tendon tics aside.

   Till now, in all our wanders, skin-to-skin
and broader sorts of shared tactility
have held firm at the barest minimum
practícable in fugitive contexts.
Frank trepidation, I confess, informs
our tacit treaty's clause obliging me.
My counterpart's deep motive, if there's one,
remains unclear, discounting stark revulsion.
(I'm not the Empire's suavest vagabond.)

   It's not impossible, you might suppose,
that, in unfathomed, couthless, limbic ways,
arousal by our newfound intimacy
now simmers his sensorium, clasped tight—
much as a twig's hugged by a desperate toad
when, in the wastes of feared Baetica,
flash floods efface topography, strip soil
and leave ravished that parched Iberian plain:
beleaguered, prostrate, languished sediment,
lascivious Spaniards with their carob staves
approaching, probing mounds of—

                           Anyhow,
be that as may, our linkage moment lends
occasion for one backbone, pillar-thick,

to flex. She braves the lapis lazuli
above, gulps three, then four voluminous
lung-loads of spumy spray and, cheerfully,
each tear gland shrieking grief, begins to trill:

> *How came we adrift in this uncharted fish drool?*
> *No foc'sle for seamen! No petrels nor pigeons*
> *to point us beachward! On this curvatured globule,*
> *no hailing Calypso, the modish Ogygian!*

"Excuse me?" I disgorge through drinks of sea.

> *Help La Agrippina! Won't some brawny swabby*
> *with pecs out to here, sweaty biceps to wrap us,*
> *come rowing at random and bélay our body*
> *along with our entourage? Where's toothless Graptus?*

"Our recent wreck's the last I saw of him."

"Well, then," the eunuch sighs, "we must write off
our slave. Make shift. Redeem ourselves. Buck up,
as Nero-Claudius-Caesar-, um, Augustus-
Germanicus's soggy momsy did.
We—rather, I—will swim for it, meanwhile
consoling selves with knowledge that the Fates
have priv'leged us to hurt identically
with Heaven's trophy, Agrippina! You
be What's-Her-Name."

           "What's whose name?"

                    "Oh, you know—

My lady-in-waiting, the one who took, smiling,
the vindictive bosun-mate's feathered plumbata
right smack in the brainpan, the meantime beguiling
his deckhands from riding me like a regatta.

"You shall be Whatsis."

"Aceronia?"

"Is that what people called her?" Spado yawns,
indifferent already. Small need's felt
to sprain emotive tendons overmuch.
No audience applauds us, anyway.

IV.

    Triremes to crush Illyria's seaboard tribes
and freighters brimmed with amber bound for home
are scarce as cliffs and sandspits in this zone
of Adriatic nowhere. (That's if, still,
we flounder in the stale backwater's spill
and aren't in Ocean's crests and troughs entrained,
to swirl until the Age of Lead descends.)

    The panorama stingily upyields
a steadily, just barely pulsing plain,
patined a weakened bilious, bronzish green,
gall-scented, too. Its seeping soundlessness
makes loud my hissing ears, both empty now,
apart from eructations, queenly boons,
allowed to slip my savior's pursèd lips,
accompanied by heard seismicities,
like scenic tourist-bait Vesuvius
when pyroclasmic viscera erupt.
Septuply-necked, self-knotted Hydras clear
digestive throats, and cause to resonate
the vast thoracic vault, against whose stays
my organ of audition's suction-cupped,
not altogether inconsolably.

    If, at this time, I weren't inhaling kelp,
I'd beg my friend to blaspheme Caesar's dam
more quietly. It's *lèse majesté*,
appalling, and endangers, though this be
a social vacuum we're dog-paddling through.
Eavesdropped upon or not, one doesn't ape,

at top of lungs, made-members of the *gens*
that lent Vergilius succor, time gone by,
while damning Ovid to that Euxine hell
for *sexualem sceleribus*.

                Fear,
as citizen, strikes me. Slow strangulation,
beheading, or judicial poison draught
awaits the pleb arraigned for blasphemy.
For stateless Spado, on the other hand,
the legal process starts with crucifixion.
Does anywhere the tree grow capable
of yielding him a pole and transverse beam
whose sturdiness remotely might suffice?

> *Are we to infer from this mastless horizon*
> *that Hope won't be heaving-to under the umbrage*
> *of paunchy Poseidon, with sea slugs bedizened?*
> *Who'll whip out his hawser and haul off my tonnage?*

"Forgive my rudeness, Spado, but your voice—"

> *Oh, Jupiter! Salvage this trusty old uterus,*
> *my wide Colosseum for gory exhibits,*
> *from which oozed the Autocrat of the Known Mundus.*
> *Except Æthiopia, Parthia, shit-pits.*

    Encouraging the subject change, I say,
"How 'bout the Land of Silk, and Indus, too?
They're never shit-pits."

                "Absolutely right—

Good point, Aceronia, brave waiting-lady!
It's plain from their dry goods that neither's a poop place:
sheer muslins, bright taffetas, pepper! Slave babies!
You're smart for a sweetie with plumbata'd brain case!

It may seem odd but, in the midst of panic,
I'm able, somehow, casually to chat.
My only strength and steadfastness, sole skill
preserving me, back home, from Princeps' penchant
for slaughter of the most insouciant sort,
was found upon my tongue's tip. Both eyeballs
can boil in sockets, heart be thumping loud
as twelve Thuringians swiving six milch cows,
and I can banter. Nothing seems amiss
beyond a nasal rising in the pitch
of my admittedly too-reedy pipes.
Such glibness under pressure on-demand's
a minor Roman virtue, I suppose.

Though lacking civic status of his own,
our castrate's no rank piker at small talk
himself, and slips as quickly into jags
of babbling as he sidles into seas.
Thus creatures of his body type are prone:

"If, graciously, I'd be the drowning momsy
of Silkies' autocrat, Indus's, too,
and savor each salt *urna* I chugged down,
d'you think I'd acquiesce to reign supreme
as Ocean Goddess, waterproof, high, dry,
of squalid Afric tribal squats, much less
those trouser-wedging, Tigris-tippling satraps
and pseudo-Persian dune sluts? No thanks, dear!
I'd sooner bite the big—"

Etcetera.
High as a flute girl's, louder than a bull's,
this diva's song, just like the rest of her,
is three-fourths falsified, one quarter real.
But let's be grateful to've grown intimate
with one unfeigned part.

Rather, make it two.

V.

Midway between the depilated armpits
and nipples, cartwheel-sized, that grandly pout
from either udder, are to be encountered
the aforementioned parts. If book-learned Greeks
at Alexandria have parsed and plumbed
anatomy's old lexicons and found,
officially, their name, I'm unaware,
yet fasten my whole personality,
unbudgeably, to such a rippling pair:
twin muscles, pudge-submerged, skull-hard handholds.

The hostess of these striate tissues hides
her flattered blushes under quaint pronouns:

> *I speak as thy sovereign's incestuous mistress,*
> *now nóblessely óbliged gently to adjure thee.*
> *Thou'lt cease and desist from thy graspings and twitches,*
> *as passersby might conceive notions unworthy—*

"What passersby? I'm trying not to die."

Such brawns, like others tendoned to Man's bones,
are imperceptible on my meek scrawn.
I've only seen them burgeoned to degrees
compárable in German conscriptees,
or mercenary spearmen, Nubians,
as mustered from detachments, caused to bear
palanquins of plump eastern client kings,
come to the capital on embassies:
a load soon eased. The dignitaries, flush

with próvincial naïveté, entrust
their diplomatic dignity and persons
(including any sunken musculature)
to present day administration's whims—
therefore, in short-lived consternation, end
dismembered, as a joke, piecemealed, then spread
posthúmously upon the throne room floor,
because Princeps finds protocol a bore.

   Their naturally perfumed Asiatic gore
gets smeared across the cunning craftsmanship
of nimble-fingered Phrygian artisans.
Red royal oleaginousness seeps
between tight breccia tiles and alabasters,
from hellish, modish caverns quarried fresh,
mosaics trimmed with agates, rosy jades
that blush like British boys' perineums,
and geometric mineral parquets
of jaspers, gravel gauds Dis Pater's sown
through Dacian ditches, Syria's wadis strewn
with renal calculi from gouty gods,
cemented seamlessly to serpentine
a toxic reptile green, plus porphyry
jammed chockablock with copper particles
to tingle Nero's foeticidal feet,
unshod for the occasion, splashing dance
'mongst unspooled oriental bowels.

                                                    His jig
is given tempi, trilled by rhythmic gales,
hydraulic laughs guffawed from brazen throats
of palisaded organ pipes, his toys,
by all Rome's ears regretted—jokesters claim,
across the broad peninsula blasted, too—

but not (Euterpe's slim twin flutes be praised)
quite loud enough to stir the Adriatic,
our present lull, where unnamed sinews save
a citizen who's pondering civic life
with half of one indifferent brain.

                              Now, if,
beneath the watered humors, deep-diffused
through plasmic serum, interstitial lymph
and "lard" (frank Pliny's dysphemistic term),
the rest of our eunuch's obése physique
is toned like my salvation-grips—or like
aforesaid mercenary Nubian's,
the spear-deploying beast whose burdened limbs
sling pre-dismembered vassals—it explains
how Agrippina's outsized replica,
with but one absent-minded backhand swipe,
in hails of teeth, rains of Neronic gore,
can knock out, cold, her slave.

                          Speaking of whom,
Graptus's mistress nips, now, nimbly, out
of character a moment, to inquire,
once more, as to her chattel's whereabouts:

  "Where is that feeble-minded mastiff fucker?"

  "I lost all sight of him, of land as well,
with something like simultaneity."

  "Then I'm compelled to throw myself, entire,
into your stout custodial care, my dear,
my loyal lady-in—what's the name again?"

"Aceronia," I labor not to sigh.

"Yes, yes, that's it. You're such a lovey-dove!
So gladly were you slaughtered to forestall
the mussing of these 'lectrum-radiant curls!"

Three upraised fingers, thick as my forearms,
twirl, primpingly, the Illyrian witch's hair
and tease away some lower sea life-forms.

This aura boils envy within Sol Invictus.
I shine him to shame at midsummer's high noontide.
His daisy beams twist in a knotted gray rictus
when heliotropy trails me, blest, blond, beaut'fied.

O'ershadowed, Sol incubates sin with some garbage
and hatches, dispatches an Oedipal bastard
(mere mooncalf: with any luck, last of our lineage)
to darken my 'do with maternal brain custard.

But you foiled his hirelings, so eagerly offering
your mousy thatch up to the pirate's plumbata
(whatever that is). How your queen's heart is soft'ning!
Snuggly Aceronia! Persona grata!

Don't think I'll forget when, together, we cower
and plead at the throne of old Rhadamanth-whoozit,
cruel Judge of the Dead, prob'ly within the hour.
I'm scaring you, aren't I? It's plain from my bruised tits.

"Best not squeeze much more earnestly than that.
Un-puncture-proof is your poor Empress Momsy,
a skin tissue, film-thin, enveloped 'round
a chassis of coagulated tears

and Eros, semi-jelled, the same as you.
(Forgive my tendency to subinduce.)

   "But, if I may speak boldly, mine's the most
unsinkable complexion west of Zeugma
by brown Euphrates' flood, where funny Bedus
inflate goat bladders taut, affixing same
on reedy rafts to lift flotation's skirts.
Then off they shove to wrangle dromedaries
that wade with suckling leeches, snuggly, sleek,
to infantile complacence lulled by sips
of camel hem'rrhage, never pinching Momsy
nor black-and-bluing teats disguised as humps.

   "That's least of countless boredom-slaughtering sights
such far-flung destinations hold in store
for tourists, jaded though our peepers be.
We'll ramble there, and further, soon, if Graptus
shows up to play the baggage boy."

                        "What bags?"

VI.

    And so on, roles and offices assigned,
rehearsed, hammed-up at leisure, while we bob,
stunned minnow-wise, through seamless green-gray-blue.
No thought nor vigor specially is bent
toward prolongation of our current lives
(or currentless—impossible to judge).
The óbese eunuch simply sculls a thigh,
perhaps affecting, once in lengthy whiles,
a languid thwartwise paddle-gesture, lazed.
A thigh-thick forearm, swishing, makes us seem
propelled, directionality of said
propulsion being single, otherwise
a matter of indifference.

                I begin
to sidestep certain wonted morbid thoughts
and entertain this possibility
(attractive to my soul's exhausted self):
the anti-embryo's counter-conception,
prerequisite to rebirth's tiresome pangs—
known otherwise as disembodiment,
metempsychotic trauma's entry wound,
as sold by Plato, bought reluctantly
by terminality-desirous me—
might not be scheduled for today.

                Just as
my hands relax a bit, Spado commences
voluptuously, and on schedule, to weep.
(One learns, with patience, to anticipate

castrati's moods distorting radically;
a wet nurse of high-average competence
could marshal mealtimes by their polar pulse.)
So down get dumped twelve steaming amphorae
of salt with moisture mingled on my head,
as if *phlégma*'s in shortage hereabouts.

> *Cry scales from your lidless eyes, roe-glutted Grecian,*
> *evictor of oysters, backwashed Aphrodite!*
> *My gill-slits are puckered with jellyfish lesions.*
> *My manservant's shark-bit or floundered, as might be!*
>
> *Was ever a Dowager douched with such dispatch?*
> *Her lungs, blotched with squid ink, are bursting asunder!*
> *She's taking on aqua by way of her bilge-hatch!*
> *Now, first of a trio of times, she goes under!*

And so she does, for drama's poignant sake:
interpretive stage business, rending hearts
contained in torsi armed with hands that clap,
expressing love for Spado, felt by whom's
a mystery to someone, dragged down too,
now shrieking bubbles, raking scarlet stripes
with fingernails, by animal reflex,
through lushness of the actress' epiderm,
dissuading her from further histrionics
that hinder respiration.

                    No one fails
to note theatric tendencies in priests
and/or priestesses consecrate, ordained
to Goddess Most Ineffable (Spado's
vocation, as you can't but have surmised).
In Anatolian precincts pots are thrown,

with antique rituals kilned, then smashed and shipped,
by crate, to far-flung missionizing outposts
deemed barbarous by cult authorities—
frontiers, backwaters, adolescent camps
(that would be Rome)—where, in novitiates,
at tenderest of ages, neophytes
(impression-prone, ardent, or merely bored,
as was the case with our friend, I suspect)
are handed one sharp shard, somehow convinced
it's piously advisable (and fun?—
why else would Spado do it?) to deprive
oneself of Nature's designated outlet
for melodrama, broad and loud: namely,
the testes, from whose normal usage flow
such howls, gyrations, grimaces and coos
as suit those midnight curbside pantomimes
abridged from vulgar freedman Terence's plays;
or seemly moans, muffled with purple wool,
befitting Senatorial marriage beds,
discreet, due spasms in *cubicula*,
where proper relict Trojans are begot,
who'll sprout, tuck gonads in their rightful place,
and do their bit to propagate the race.

   The Goddess's clergy, sliced, are rendered prone,
through residues of so-called "natural lives"
(no more man-made than mine, in other ways),
to affectations of unsubtle sorts.
In social-climbing mode, these sacred castrates,
obese, emaciate, or in between,
will tone it down, attempting to affect
effete aestheticism. They aspire
to rarefied estates of wealthy pathics
who, swathed transparently in silken gauze

with corals pink as sphincters spangling hems,
have draped their recta 'round the Palatine
since accession of the mad incendiary.

    At slight or less-than-niggling provocation,
they're pleased to mount impromptu personations
of worthies resurrected from old times,
with two provisos: phalli disallowed,
and naughtiness stretched well beyond the "norm"
(if the latter term elicits more than shrugs
since Augustus' missus fed him doctored figs).
Medea, butcheress of kith and kin,
still hawks her unguents, this time in the baths.
Semíramis, famed pony fornicator,
in counterfeit trots 'round the arena's rim,
to neigh at splinter-Hebrews, "Lions' lunch!"
Our own hometown's nymphomaniacal
doyenne of misbehavior, Messalina,
posthúmously transgresses through the fora,
as Anarch of the Night. Meanwhile, at sea,
our matricide of an Imperator's
dead parent pours bad lady aconite
into my ear, commixed with honeyed drips.

    We saddened throwbacks to the manned Republic,
from several blocks and porticoes away,
can hear these smooth-crotched functionaries swish,
exerting no-wise to distinguish selves
from "artists," who of late un-Hellenize
our Italian stage with bosoms falsified,
falsetto squawks and unfeigned flatulence.
They prance the boards with Agrippina's son,
until upstaging, in some feckless lust,
their Emperor—equivalent offence

in Nero's so-called "mind" to parricide.
And if he doesn't mince them straight away—
a lusis for the matinee that day,
deus ex bodkin—their due penalty,
as meted (on and off) since Tarquin's time,
is Tiber drowning, stitched into a bag,
tough oxhide, with a small menagerie:
one specimen from each broad family
of mindless creatures, feathered, scaled and furred.
An ape's included—but no trout or carp.
(It's simply too bizarre, even for Caesar,
inventive though he be, to juxtapose
a fish with our municipal sewage sluice.)

    If, with permission and apologies,
I may attempt another simile—
that crowded sack is like my incarnation,
the coat of skin I'm loath to see unsewn,
with reptile, carrion buzzard, matted brute,
my triple gnashers toward internal doom.
Downriver, in some rank, malarial swamp,
their claws and fangs will breach my leathern womb.
This parent-killer, birthed, will recommence
the overlabored pun called "existence,"
unless a timely rescue is arranged
upon the execution of my sentence,
my flinging from the Pons Sublicius.

    Will You-Know-Who, just by coincidence,
come side-stroking luxuriantly by,
idly negotiating Rome's supply
of culinary muck? Will I, between
the cinchèd sutures of embodiment,
untangle thumb and fingers, pecked and mauled,

to grab his and/or her lifesaving ribs?
Will we, castrato with oxskin conjoined,
descend to Tiber's spreading estuary,
confettied with bright-sailed, salvific boats?
Remote from culpable Illyria,
soon shed of ribboned souvenirs therefrom,
will we lave us in the brisk Tyrrhenian
and surf the breakers with assorted pets?

VII.

"Know what, Spado—I mean, Agríppina?"

Magnanimous, Her Highness condescends
to grant me license: "Speak."

                      "If you're not dead,
you cannot—"

"Silence down there!"

                           "—be divine.
Perhaps you should recall that, legally,
your son could only have you deified
and niche your bust amid the pantheon
with flowers, frankincense, combusting doves,
subséquent to your slaughter. But today
you're proving such a swimmer, without peer—"

"Of course. The Naiads covet my breast-stroke."

"—that Nero must resort to thugs and cudgels
impinging on the godhead candidate
once swum ashore, toweled off, retired, abed,
between her purple pillows fluffed and tucked,
asleep, high and—"

              "—not necessarily dry.
Yet here I am, undrowned, unclubbed, unbedded
(unfortunately) and divine, all one.
And you're my lady-in-blah blah, What's-Her-Face,

who only speaks when spoken to. Besides,
you've got the bosun-matey's oaken oar
sunk in your sallow, furrowed, mousy brow."

   "I thought you said it was a plumba—"

                                        "Oar.
Your brains are spilling iridescent slicks
and unctuous films of Aceronian gore
to grime our mobile Adriatic isle.
So much for you. Where's Graptus infant-gums?
How dare he leave me unattended here?"

   "He's vanished. Your valet's—"

                               "—slouched underneath
the featureless horizon's lonesome throb."

   The seascape's scanned, bereavement mused upon.
We're plunged in a moroseness so abrupt
I'm nearly flung wide of our situation,
like tradesmen thrown by balking donkeys.

                             "Ah!
can I recall a time when simple Graptus
did not manage my personal hygiene?"

   She moans, sucks lips, re-spigots on the weeps,
albeit dutifully, a smidgen bored.
Then melancholy trance evaporates
like moisture sublimated straight to aether,
and gruff he waxes, gravel-voiced (as far
as able in his ill-equipped condition).
With all the rough affect of mannish types,

or Stoic stalwarts too top-brimmed with virtue
to yield a sigh for grief's effeminacy,
in bass (or maybe baritone) he burps—

"Damn Graptus' eyes, har-*rummph*—"

"—har-what?"

"You heard me.
Stout lad, though, all in all. Far better man
than—well, no need to grease it overmuch.
So, now, un-slaved indignity's imposed.
Henceforth our way's self-wrought—to where? Who knows?—
with no pack animal to tease, trip, kick
and mock, beguiling tedium of the trudge.
Not that we've much impedimenta left.
The larcenous seabed's fully stocked today—
except for my, er, handsome, rugged, butch
toupée, up top, right here, just so, wedged tight.
Oh, yes, and—"

Girlish grins traverse the face,
a mile across, that, gibbous as a moon,
imposes on me.

"—not to mention, dear—"

She nudges underwater with an elbow
that jostles me from shoulder to mid-shin.

"—a certain entry in our inventory—"

I'm winked at.

      "—a memento, fetched as well
from weird Illyria, and far too dear
for strapping luggage-wise amid our kit
on rickety slaveling's swayback shoulder blades,
to plummet hellward with the drudge himself
at slightest hint of dampness—that is, if
you take my meaning when I, gigglingly,
up-curl my lips, crinkle my silly nose
and circumlocute, coyly lisping hints,
thin-veiled, of our beloved item."

        Wink
again, with vortices of squishing sounds
from satchel-sized eyelids.

       The hint's received.
Full knowledge of that "item's" boundless worth
informs, enflames my mind, and rapes my soul
as well, because, like Graptus, it's been lost.
Unloosing my salvation-grips, I fall,
as if no sea's up-buoying us, through cold
parched emptiness, to tumble toward the trench
that bottomlessy sucks upon our heels.

 Guess who was charged with holding that one thing.

VIII.

 The sanguine picture of the universe
enjoyed, surprisingly, by Spado's ilk
(that is, when not bewailing pendent doom)
allows the eunuch glibly to assume,
regarding said particularity
(a jar, to be precise), that no mere shipwreck
could fluster, feminize, de-Romanize,
or weaken, otherwise, my arms; and that
our second keepsake of Illyria
(the one not made of human body parts)
remains secreted, firm, about my person,
befitting a just cosmic dispensation;
and I've not been misdeemed reliable
by our Priest of the Most Ineffable,
about whose person's presently secreted,
in turn, my own person: ergo, Spado
now labors under misassumption's yoke,
and overestimation of his leech,
as, otherwise, he'd feel the stoneware, cool,
against his altered loins. For guilt unspeeched,
I can't relieve him of such baseless cheer.

 Extended concentration's no strong point
among those sporting emptied scrotal sacs
(no doubt, like dropsied thighs, a side effect).
Back in, back out again of her butch mode,
she trills, "D'you mind if I go wee-wee much?
Yes? Maybe? No? Please ask me if I care."

And, that encompassed, Spado speculates
extempore historiography,
apostrophizing Aceronia:

> *You teaser! Forever great thinkers and knowers*
> *will ask if you proffered your skull in the struggle,*
> *or tried to fellate that mean horsey-hung rower.*
> *You minx! Did you hanker for smooth or rough snuggles?*

"Don't tell me. You're about to say, 'Perhaps
my darling waiting-lady's game for both.'"

"Luck of the draw, and all that sort of thing."

"And paid the price."

                "Or garnered the reward."

"A plumb—I mean, an oar creasing the brow
comprises her reward?"

                "You never know,"
my large friend leers. "That final gasping breath
could be a brain-upending orgasm,
the kind that makes Goddess Ineffable
get moist and grunt. A ruffian's oaken tool
may feel much nicer, deep inside your noggin,
than any scrumptious tidbit in your tummy,
e.g., a perfect mushroom, red, with spots
of white, breast-stroking bright Hyblean honey—
if, as before, you take my meaning."

                Nudge
plus wink. Her meaning's taken, once again.

My heart, already fallen to the bottom,
begins to burrow in the sediment
to hide for shame beneath the sardine stools.
Please guess what spore-plump tidbits, kept from rot
by bee secretions, fulfilled our lost pot.

    Comes Spado's giggle: "That Neronic boatman
is navigating someone's tiny head.
D'you feel his punting paddle, that wet wood,
those salty knots, those splinters, spongy, cool,
slough up against your brain-bone's inner wall,
comprising, Aceronia, your reward?"

"You're drifting into climes where I can't breathe."

"Yes, we salvation cultists have boned up
on speculation, eschatology
and morbid chattiness. Speaking of such,
you've salvaged our jarred kissy-'shrooms, correct?"

    Lucky for me, our dame's sanguinity
compels no need to linger for reply.

> *Let's gobble one each, which, for me (skin atingle),*
> *in practical terms, tallies up a half-dozen*
> *sweet lovelies. For you, that's exactly a single,*
> *if you're a real Stoic and won't try to cozen.*
>
> *We'll need nourishment for our jaunt to hell's storage*
> *where lackeys, presuming they're freed, lounge like lizards.*
> *Mine's lazing around, brain dissolving to porridge.*
> *My soul will re-kill his with chops to the gizzard.*

Tom Bradley

    A downward swiping of the monstrous hand
with which he means to halve a menial
whose wholeness is already compromised
(symbolic gesture, meant to edify
myself more than to disconcert the ghost,
ostensible in any case, of Graptus)
gets answered by a tidal wave, the first
perturbing of the liquid, now our home.

    A sand-grain rinsed from Neptune's navel, I
must surely shriek more bubbles. Extra stripes
with animalistic fingernails are raked
in Spado, who applauds my histrionics.

IX.

    I shriek not for life-loss, but that of fungus.
I scratch for mushrooms, gone. Eaten, they turn
the heavens inside-out, switch situations
with Pluto's morgue, and backward-somersault
behind my orbits. Unassuming man
though I might be, my tunic gets unloosed,
my tongue, too, by these red, white food-like things.
As never's been my wont, I strain the reeds
that squeak in my un-Roman neck, and blast,
along with Spado, through this unlawed Empire—

    Fuck all in the world unconducive to chuckling—
    which means nearly nothing beneath Sol's pink pucker!
    If risible muscles in cheeks are not buckling
    with spasms, they're unworth their jaws' infrastructure!

    Our grocer was the witch, abovementioned,
whose pelt of flaxen ringlets seems foredoomed
to be the singularity redeemed
from sheer calamity, heartbreak, disaster
upon the high seas, earlier today.
I disenjoy that screeching crone as topic,
and won't exposit her, except to say
what, surely, you'll already have surmised:
the practical (i.e., the manual)
particularities of Spado's truck
with said Illyrian were Graptus' tasks.
Do call us social climbers if you'd like,
but eunuchs with their nurslings ever strive
to follow old philosophy's advice:

the gentleman should never touch a tool.
So, wig procurement, also preparation,
peruker's offices, must be fulfilled
by servile members of one's "touring troupe,"
as Spado calls us when he's getting bored
with "Empress and her flunkies" metaphors.

    To speak in frankness, we resemble more
a pack of fugitives, to slim extent
that legal status technically remains
achievable in sagging Pax Romana.
A lax administrator, the assassin
of Agrippina smirks at brigandage
and piracy's resurgence.

                  "We could use
resurging pirates, two or three, 'round here.
I'll have a smirked-at brigand on the side,
a hung one—and I don't refer to crosses,
three nails and droopy swaddles. Maybe swaddles."

    With no response forthcoming from below,
upon his ox-yoke collarbones Spado
compresses numerous chins. He aims his face
straight downward. For the first time in our lives,
he looks at, maybe in, my eye, or eyes.
With sounds neither unnaturally low
nor freakish-high, but in his rightful, smooth,
cool countertenor comes a croon:

                   "I hope
your neck's not craned to scrutinize the Earth's
nude curvature for Graptus evidence."

"He could catch up."

          "Sea monsters have defleshed
our tyke already, bootless as that sounds,
like this sardine whose ribs accentuate
my blond bouffant."

          "Many of the unfree
are dilatory, systematically,
as to postpone our working them to death."

"I never worked that slug a solid day—

> *He's deader than Momsy in bed, bloodied, cudgeled.*
> *He came at a bargain, like bug-riddled lumber,*
> *for this is the way of the Mundus. Befuddled?*
> *Consult any priest, scrotally unencumbered.*
>
> *I guarantee Graptus, cut-rate, deep-discounted,*
> *dissolved with our boat. Just like you, he was leaky.*
> *We swim in him now, mucous membranes surrounded*
> *with slave gravy—gross thought! One tightens one's cheekies.*

X.

    It's gross, yes, but well taken, Spado's point
anent his bondman's solubility.
The drudge's muscle tone befitted boys,
his fat-stores all but nonexistent, skin
that rashed upon his brittleness green-gray,
a grandpa shade. Old Pliny classifies
that constellation of pathologies
specific to unfortunates nursed, weaned
and reared upon a jejune acorn diet
in regions scrounged where agriculture's lore
has yet to attain the currency of rumor,
from whose (speak frankly) barely bestial bourne
a rooting runt named Graptus might be snatched.

    "He may have been half-hog food," Spado says,
"but not a precious mushroom. Don't anoint
the slouch in produce of industrious hives.
Let this be Graptus' mealy threnody:
in spirit botched, in bowels deficient, he,
to sum with single derogation, was—"

    "Illyrian."

        "That's right."

                Spado's pack mule
shared species with the master's source of coif.
Illyria's drizzle incubates such languor
within its half-jelled bloodlines, one assumes
the formerly towheaded sorceress

was Graptus' vague tribeswoman, maybe aunt,
who hawked him into bondage, time gone by.

    No brawn of which to boast, wan, bony scrawn,
not quite "the Empire's suavest vagabond"—
is that familiar? Add a reedy voice?
Mere superficial semblance, little more.
A twin wandering that Adriatic shore
may rue similitude with Spado's pet,
but not your narrator. Italian, me,
from the proper side of this defining sea.
Un-familied with steppers, strange to fetchers,
of balding conjuresses kith nor kin,
I'll not let debased acorns grease my chin
(except polenta mush, deemed civilized,
permissible cuisine, when wheaten harvests,
and those of spelt and emmer, barley, oats,
are proved substandard); nor do I intend
to retrogress as Graptus substitute,
if one's required. (Self-sworn's a tacit oath
to that effect.)

        And neither am I versed
in haggles, barters, hustles, cons and thefts
of coastal Adriatic substance mongers.
I'm left no recollection to be shared
of business transacted. All's erased.
As Dowager's predesignated taster,
it fell on me, with tentative gustation,
to take between my teeth mycology
of probable toxicity. Flat naught's
remembered after that—except to note,
with cranial shudders, true complexity
of texture, broad bouquet beyond the reach

of uninitiate sense. The province's
sole product of appreciable value, strange
brain-foodstuffs, with disinterest compared,
make cool Falernian, vintaged under sway
of timeliest frosts to kiss Campania,
galumph one's uvula like lukewarm whey.

    One's poisoning's preemption, normally,
would be the slave's prerogative. But waste
it seemed to us, or outright sacrilege,
redundantly to cast the fungal spell
on Graptus' "mind" (forgive the word's abuse).
The unfree consciousness, as self-betrayed,
is rudimentary at its optimum,
and likely whiles its non-perspiring time
awash in demon-swarming stupors, such
as we free men approximate, but briefly,
by seeking and consuming backwoods philters,
coarse compounds, barbarous, rank, raw, witchified:
Hyblean-syruped gills, plump sporocarps
with stippled pílei of lurid blush,
on ithyphallic stipes, annuli-cinched,
stiff stemmage plunged in volvae, lipped in mulch
as "fruiting bodies," plus—

                      What's better named,
taxonomized with sheerer lingo-glee?
Your Elder Pliny, cataloguing, drowns
in salivation mouthing 'shroom syllabics!
Your Alexandrian Greeklings, with this drool,
can spigot Nilic floods if drought descends
to desiccate the Æthiopes' shit-pit,
too arid for my mycoid muse to smooch!

Approximating stupors swarmed with "demons"
(what pass for such in numb Illyria),
with crystal clarity I can't recount
comeuppance of the close-cropped beldam. Thanks
to honeyed scamps, white stars on their red caps,
my memory of the hag's tonsure coheres
less tightly than our wrecked "ship's" seams (or joints?),
once Graptus stacked the deck with us, our kit
and Auntie's pelt—which, I've come to suspect,
is cursed. A supernatural agency
explains the inexplicability
of planks to pulp degraded in a blink.

    Our touring troupe's authority on things
of spirit, deep religion's subtleties,
the castrato-priestess can't but be aware
of any maledictions she might bear
sunbonnet-wise—but Spado doesn't care.
The bitterest, most efficacious hex
secreted through the hollowed, beauteous fangs
of swine-confecting Circe on her isle
and launched from that shrill sea into this swamp,
must, like a mud-bred minnow, ricochet
off my cetaceous friend's vitality.

    I'm safer 'round my óbese eunuch wrapped
than tucked amidships on a mile-long freighter,
with worlds of cereal stocked and stabilized,
Ostía-bound, in dreams of perfect weather.

XI.

To talk of vessels sliding on the sea,
a plank, not quite degraded into pulp,
but melted, flaccid, maybe from our boat,
now sloshes toward my arm's periphery.
A bit of wooden business, up it floats
self-deprecatingly, just soft enough
to sneak beneath the óbese eunuch's ken
and damply into contact-nudge with me.

On second thought, it might not be a board,
this gloppy thing, identifiable,
just barely, as a crumb, an afterthought
of previous circumstance. If it be wood,
its splinters feel too spongy, look to writhe
a bit, not much—no cause for huge surprise
were mushrooms, makers of your sight to squirm,
consumed and not mislaid. Seesawing slow
upon the wavelets, ripples, licks and laps
that pass for tides in Adriatic calms,
this mass of bubbles, grief and seaweed starts,
with consciousness, or so it seems, to tap
me on the disbelieving shoulder blade.

"Good gracious!" Spado trills, oblivious—

> *We're peckish between the earlobes, Aceronia.*
> *Unwedge the sweet mushy-jar from your vagina*
> *and plunge wrist bone-deep in the bug-brewed ambrosia.*
> *Our lady-in-can't-wait! Let's roust Proserpina!*

It's my turn now to augment Adriatic
with squirts of orbit-brine wrung from my face,
decanted not in Empress-deep amphorae,
but drips of *ligulae*, proportional.

My crying's small, cathartic nonetheless,
as, secondhand, we're taught by Spado's colleague
in priestly nontesticularity:
the self-styled "Semirámis Redivivus."
Committed flagellant, religious seeker,
she slums amid the offshoot-Hebrew cult
who, in the Colosseum's bustling wings,
while waiting turns to nourish carnivores,
will preach salvific properties of tears
in settling eschatology's arrears.
So do I now, like Chrestiani, wail,
but with discretion, swallowed, Roman-style:
preemptive penance for my imminent breakage
of our castrato's continent-sized heart,
my un-victualing his famished mental maw;
atonement for the fumbling of provisions,
jarred provender, now lost, uncheaply bought
with misbehavior, inexpìable.

My lamentation's understated, Stoic,
nor moistly do I squawk, like a capon
who flits about the sin-beleaguered city
of my despicable nativity,
abashèd not to crave, solicit, seek
chastisement, as it's sternly meted out
by reborn Messalina, Night's Anarch.
Her hips, strapped, wield a tastelessly outsized,
grain-dyed Pompeiian-red leathern *baubón*,
with artisanal smoothness sunken-stitched,

anointed in the olive's intimate unction.
Some sediment's unstrained, by paradox,
to lend a friction-hint, perhaps promote,
in teaseful modicum, internal chafes
of membranes, ill-advised, unless—

                                              My point
is taken, I presume—but not by Spado.
He's unaware that I don't brim with bliss
commensurate with his. (Admittedly,
that's saying nearly nothing: as you've seen,
my traveling companion sets the mark
for self-absorption in the ranks of bipeds
who strut, eschewing benefit of feathers—
at least the pins that come pre-plunged in pores.)

   Without awareness, I commence repining,
at top of lungs, a hybrid Spadic stanza:

> *Why didn't blue Neptune grab Graptus' great-auntie's*
> *effeminate scalp and ignore her nutritious*
> *parfait of red toadstools, permitting us scanty*
> *provisions, more sticky, but less unpropitious?*

   "Excuse me, honey? Didn't quite catch that.
You need to hack the kelp from your cute craw
before orating so adorably.
I hope that's not soliloquy already.
There's ample time for blabbed delirium
when your slim carcass comes to cotton on:
no potability moistens her prospects."

XII.

    Dehydrated or not, I carry on
self-mortifying, splinter-Hebrew-style—
or try to. That ambiguous intruder,
memento mori from our joke-boat, keeps
distracting me from weeps, hovering about
to smear salt globules of its weedy self,
half-pulp, half-plank, upon my spine, my nape,
my armpit, tapping tempo with that slosh,
maintaining in its spongy nudges time,
tribo-magnetic rhythmics unexpected
in currentlessness of the present sea.
The flotsam's importunacy might feel
with microcosmos rather synchronized
than with the hydrospheric pulse, as if
this accidental wad of wood, or mind,
or protoplasm's sprouted sentience,
a heart and lungish gills, albeit malformed.
Aborted foetal baby boat, it bops,
again and over yet again, against
the bones of my all-too apparent frame.
I fear relinquishing salvation grips
for manual repulsion. One might blow
contrary bubbles toward the undulate mess,
but that requires my lips' double descent
into the reeking exudate it makes,
this twin of mine in uterine regression.

    Spado could make it disappear, no doubt:
a single glaring of her eye, sunned mildew.
But circumstances cannot call her down.

Tom Bradley

Our former craft, residuum thereof,
could founder in the Milky Way and she
would hail no higher heavenward than now.
She feels no taps, no nudges—naught beyond
myself, to which she sinuously responds:

> *So, what's with the honey jar? Momsy's mouth waters,*
> *as do her mind-glands. Other bits of her belly*
> *aren't drought-stricken, either. Your knee, in its wanders,*
> *probes ártesian aquifers. Aqua Patella!*

Embarrassed, I'd withdraw, if open sea
weren't all there'd be to sunder her and me.

Characteristic absentmindedness
dismisses hinge joints from her world. She says—

> *I'm thinking of banishing Graptus' ass homeward*
> *to Trans-Adriatic. The spastic hangs back as,*
> *in peripeteia (is that the Greek loan-word?),*
> *we fall to where momsies get damned in a fracas.*

"No point in asking where that is of me,
mere priestess of salvation cultishness:
perhaps 'the Underworld'—or, as my dupe
is schooled to call it, *After*world. That fine
distinction makes him slightly less morose
while wasting one existence catching farts.
At all events, fuck him. I know I did,
but numerously. 'Shroomy-womby time!'"

XIII.

    Our small flotilla now unfocuses
behind my penitent Chrestiani tears.
A real shipwreck, like the obstetric horror
that dumped Aeneas in Queen Dido's lap,
would not excuse such infantility.
The castrate's spirit, not to mention mine,
is doomed to fade from malnutrition, thanks
to me, stout citizen of peerless Rome.
Just as the missing vessel, topside, bore
a seal composed of elm sap kneaded thick
with forest floor detritus, tendrils, twigs,
so am I stoppered with a plug of pride.
There's nothing for it but to open me,
a breached receptacle. Drink lethal draughts.
Inhale the amniotic gall, rebirth's
funereal unguent. Grease the next abyss.
Turn loose each transsexed sinew and consign
contemptibility to finny deeps.
High time, yet once again, for me to go.

    But, expectation shocked, the Goddess' priestess
by one pinched ear defers my drowned demise,
reversing an odd process splinter-Jews
are seen subjecting one another to
in drainage ponds. Creation's airy half
is what she pulls me up into, so far,
at least, as windpipe goes. One could suppose
she'd rather not, in perpetuity,
be set adrift without my company.

"Sad lady, what's your silly name again?"

"Aceronia?"

"No, that's not it. Really?"

Not only inlets to the lungs uplift,
but vaults and catacombs of heart as well.
A relic of the Republic, my staunch self,
much more than merely edified, is blest
by Spado, Prophet-Revelator-Seer,
this triply sanctified conduit, mirror
of She-God's inexpressibility:
remotely antique Anatolia's
profoundest dispensation, in whose glow
togati are exposed as bully bumpkins.
Engaging an apotropaic arm
to anchor, prayerfully, my languishment
to his unsinkabilty, my friend
delivers, ransoms, manumits, affords
new respiration, unpersuading me
from selfhood-slaughter's brink.

This Holy Man
(this Holy Person, rather) showers boons
to tide me till life's rigmarole resumes.
A castrato carved of cork, redemption breaks
the surface tension, fizzes, hymning, up
to bob beneath the dry cerulean.
A slumber-desecrating bosun-matey's
plumbata (handily doubling as an oar),
though swung by brawn imperially engaged,
must carom off a brow felicitous,
a sinciput new-christened, like my own.

Once breath's been caught, "Yes, Aceronia,"
I'm heard to say.

    The gloried gelding chucks
my under-chin. She jounces nursery jigs:

> *A whimsical name for a loyal, brave, dowdy*
> *and mousy twit-twat with a mean paddly-waddly*
> *all pokey-pooed smack in her low, wrinkly, pouty*
> *pink monkey-brow—ooh! There's no need to sing sadly!*

I'm squeezed to squeaking like an ape unstitched
from a bag of overcrowded baby-pets.

In Spado's inborn countertenor tones
a cryptic oracle's arcanely crooned:

> *Chromatical puzzle suggestive of something:*
> *a monkey with red face, white spots, like boys' bad skin,*
> *but colors reversed, as to meld youth's first stippling*
> *with flushed hypertension decrepitude basks in.*
>
> *A paradox: pimply yet wrinkly complexion,*
> *a red thing, a white thing, that, overnight sprouted,*
> *contains, in stomata, myths aged beyond reckon,*
> *a contradiction with gustation about it.*
>
> *Up-snouters of acorns, like Graptus the Illyrian,*
> *exude both bizarreries, plus each opposed scent:*
> *the Cumaean Sibyl in fungussy caverns,*
> *perpetually babyish, meanwhile senescent.*

"Yes, Elder Pliny has a chapter on—"

"Ah, me. So sad. She reads old Know-It-All.

My dugs, doubly bruised in two pigments specific
to hemm'rhage besprinkled with splotches of pustules,
contusions sucked up by your novitiate nerve-tics,
are dropping you broad hints of honey-sunk toadstools.

Elbow-dimensioned knuckles wipe my lids,
expecting me to peek into a jar,
instead enabling me, with more than nostrils,
too-shrill tactility and hissing ears,
to test the jetsam that impinges, still,
upon the freshly counter-baptized me.

XIV.

    Redemption's no castrato carved of cork,
as it turns out. A different artifact,
contrasting in its physical properties,
delivers bliss. Not featherweight or porous,
but vitrified, green-glazed, kilned and—no thanks
be to the Goddess unto whom testes
are rendered up—intact, unlike the tool
of Spado's ordination. Into sight,
as if on cue, fortuitously it heaves,
tucked snug upon that sorceress-blasted blob
of un-boat. Rockish superfices flash
with sunshine, hinting dreams that might attend
ingestion of its contents. Elm sap seal
hymenally unchallenged, it arrives,
improbable coincidence, godsent,
pure providence, rewarding signal valor
displayed in nautical adversity
by me: the selfsame singular container
for whose perdition I'd self-castigate
and play the low-down seabed annelid.

    The forty-ninth Nereid, prettiest, best
of all her half a hundred sisters, blessed
our snacks and fetched them here to nourish thoughts,
disguised as component of flotsam gush.
Profundities I hear the mycoid choir
too sweetly chant in their ceramic shrine.

    "Let's make ourselves into a chuckling pair
of fruiting bodies, Adriatic-style,"

says Spado, not commenting on my find,
of which he stays oblivious, too high
with mania to leave uneyed the sky.
"Let's smirk indecently at sporocarps.
I'm ready for refreshments 'round 'bout now!"

    Behind the wayward pot a thing's in tow,
hardly describable, except, perhaps,
with that vague modifier, favored still
among Palatine pathics: *off-putting*.
Entangled, dragging in the non-plank's wake
of saline gel, a semi-entity—
or maybe just a slick of ruddy grease,
spread thin, dilute—presents with certain hints
of animation, more or less. Tissues
of frayed and hempen rags are raveled, snagged
in broken bits of tree corpse. If alive,
halfhearted at the most; if fully dead,
inconsequential—though, it seems to groan.

    This will be dealt with later. I decide
exclusively to ponder sea nymphs, not
the cyclopés who dog their sodden steps.
I'll ride this wave till it unwinds in ringlets
and comes unribboned on a civil beach.

XV.

    Too busy feigning Empress Momsyhood
to note miraculous recoveries
of fungal jam preserves, the emasculee
throat-chortles up and down three modal gamuts,
to sing a jar she only sees in mind.

    "I'm jealous, 'cause my beefy mitt won't fit.
You must feed me, much like a lissome lynx
in Rome's municipal menagerie."

    My travel-mate employs a single arm
to achieve such oratorical effects
as cleaving Neptune's fearful element,
gesticulating orisons to Jove
and twining fondled spit curls 'round her thumb.
Her other limb about my corpus spirals,
thus freeing my ten fingers from her thews,
should I turn loose (non-suicidally
this time) to unseal any earthenware
that might be navigating lazily by.

    "Don't let me grow impatient, now, dearie.
You know how fretful-pettish I can get
when wants and whims aren't instantaneously
indulged, fed, gratified and met. I pout,
like this—"

    She wrenches gorgon grimaces.

"Sometimes I even slap!"

                        She feints a stroke
athwart the flinching Heavens overhead.
No tidal wave this time.

                        I must confess
succumbing to a pair of slavish urges
that couldn't contradict with meaner baseness
the manlier precepts of our Stoic saints:
low gluttony and shifty furtiveness.
Again without the eunuch taking note
(his eyes are closed in thespianic rapture),
I scrape from the repository's rim
some shreds of what resembles lower bowel
(familiar sight to eyes that scorn to blink
procedures in the Colosseum's ring).
I crack the stopper—lending half an ear,
or less, to the off-putting, tangled mass,
whose moans are sounding like a loaded M-word:
a plaintive *Master*, or perhaps *Mistress*.

  It's due to castaways' malnourishment,
the belly's emptiness deranging sense
(a safe, or not, assumption), but, before
my eagerness can stretch a single thumb
into adhesiveness, before one gill,
piléus, annulus, volva or stipe
can come within my lips' vicinity,
on strength, alone, of mushrooms' viscid vapor
up-seeped from this mélange into my nose,
the sea, with snap-instantaneity,
like aspic on a salver, jiggles once,
then vanishes, a vacuum, clarified
as Alpine atmosphere in month of Maius.

Useful Despair

    Without my wonted squint, I apprehend,
from miles above, between four hovering feet,
an open seabed laid with opal shards
and amethyst: dry submarine parquet
that minerally shells the Mundane Egg,
recursing more abstruse geometry
than Nero's hemorrhagic throne room floor,
but similarly heaped with piecemealed life.
I catalogue and scrutinize the rinds
of starfish, stingrays, squids and skeletized
Illyrians who've slunk too close to shore.
Come whales of vertigo, compounding horror
that, given minor alterations, might
be tightened into sheer spinal delight.

    Just as anticipation's fixed to fetch
my spored confection, dotted bonbon-treat,
as if to compensate for perfect lack
of weather in the sky (where it belongs),
a cloud, peculiar-colored, now obscures
our hypo-panorama, billows 'round
extremities, enshrouds umbilicus,
submerges chin, then infiltrates the mouth,
then snout, amazement-gaped, to register,
like gore in panic shed, the smoke and tang
of steely rust.

        Those rare softhearted plebes
who don't avail themselves of Rome's arena,
the combats and the feedings of big cats,
will tend to call this tincture "coppery,"
while worldwise men who've witnessed aunties cured
of dandruff permanently, know too well
expiring iron's hard aroma. Hence

the redness, as opposed to greenish tinge
of veins' embarrassment—presumably
of this opacity as well. Its source
would seem environed by the fractured plank,
or thinking thing, whatever it might be
that's sailed the cause of thoughts like these to me.

   Into the straits between us gentlemen
this flightless nimbus self-insinuates,
and lathers charter members of our troupe
with scarlet-russet froth, gritty yet slick,
much like the contradictory lubricant
ameliorating Messalina's dildo,
but not expressed from blameless olive pulp.

   I hear myself step out of character
to offer up this quip:

>   "And here I've been
projecting dry menopausality
on our kakistocrat's beloved dam."

   "What are you blabbing now? Blaspheming me?"

   Spado's obesity begins to wax,
the volume of her voice to swell—

>   "I am
that sacrosanct and reverend She!"

         Something
persuades me, once again, to focus sense
upon the gloppy thing's amorphousness.
It flounders on one side, like grim sardines

in Naples Bay, well-hooked but unreeled in,
because the angler's choked by brimstone passed
from Mount Vesuvius' inverted ass.
It quickens yet expires. Something puckered
about this floater, gilled and semi-hatched,
curled-up and crumbly, puts me in off-mind
of uterine detritus sloughed from dames
with overbearing tendencies: half-tykes
in stages of non-viability;
Illyrian youngsters, honeycomb-diseased,
laid, flattened, cribbed beneath the forest moss,
the un-Italian endometria
of vegetative subhumanity.

   These nonsequential notions, coalesced
into a single urging—one flatfish
that nuzzles sacral vertebrae—convey
themselves osmotically up to our gelding.
The moister aspects of maternity
into his vocalizing seep, as he
continues growing fatter, taller, louder—

   "Magnificence am I, who whelped and swived
her murderer 'twixt soon-avenging thighs!"

   Time for a certain someone to dig in.

XVI.

    Some slippery, sticky fungus-honey helps
and hinders, up to knob of wrist, my fist
to waylay more than the allotted single
of tidbits' numinosity, whose crunch
will coincide with mushy contradiction:
a complex texture, bouquet similar
to what I mouthed when, back on Terra Firma,
in quasi-servile status was employed
praegustator to pseudo-Agrippina.
This taste has its olfactive complement
in hogos heaving up behind the plank—
as if the semi-entity, damp snag,
springs also from transadriatic dirt,
twin parasitic growth upon decay:
selfsame Illyrian species as this plant,
great-nephew to a masticating aunt.

    The redness, not to mention raggedness,
now registers upon my nose, and brings
increasing recognizability
to ears, growing decipherability.
The groans assume some rudimentary vowels
and half-tongued consonants, like those that drool
from gums of tiny toddling stranger-beings
conceived, gestated, given parturition
with steadily decreasing frequency
by Senators who blithely disobey
Lex Julia et Papia-Poppaea.

Tom Bradley

    Again, this time in baby-talk, is moaned
the M-word, masculine and feminine
declensions interchanged, or merely muddled.

    As if on cue, the Dowager crescendos—

>   *D'you hear me rejoicing in having neglected*
>   *to strangle my matricide, offspring and bunk mate,*
>   *garotted umbilically, windpipe transected,*
>   *his fontanelle flattened by labial uptake?*

    The lips in question wrench impressively,
in tempo, on the final substantive.
I feel them pucker through the fecund brine:
enunciation, fair; embouchure, fine;
good muscular control where no such thews
can, in the strictest terms, be said to flex,
unlike the ripplers bolstering his chest.

XVII.

    For this account to retain rigor, here
let's pause a moment prior to swallowing 'shrooms
and clarify: the vulva Spado boasts
between his two conveyances, dropsied,
eléphantine, and cultivates with pride,
is rather more a matrix of scar flaps,
with Greekling surgeon's cleverness bedraped
around a mèatus somewhat more pronounced
than that which drains your average plebeian.
(I'm privy to this all-essential lore
because we're travel partners, nothing more.)
He likes to call his idiosyncrasy
"the Grand Imperatrix's *cicatrix*,"
a Pliny word I plundered for the purpose,
in place of the misnamed "venereal *mons*."

    My mind knows this. My knee's experience
will beg to contradict, to dare nay-say
our mother: neither artificial wound
nor rebirth's vent. My sharp patella's jammed
unhappily against an undulation,
a differentially configured zero.

    This opposite fanged vacancy, crammed, too,
with surfeited existence, starts to belch—
not queefs, but burpings—oceanic suds
of womb gas that engulf my head and pop,
with snickers first, then growls, then gnashing screams,
evolving gradually to parent talk—

*Why didn't I squinch up my gloried quim-sphincter
when Nero, the future Divine Empress-trouncing
brat-bastard broke water, far better extincter?
Why didn't I snap off his cap when first crowning?*

*How bouncy and fun would be poxy Romana,
if not for that foetus' continued excrescence
and silly, endearing, naïve Agrippina's
forgivable lack of political prescience!*

Down there spurts no "artesian aquifer."
My kneecap's bopping canines and incisors—
unsprung from fabled *vagina dentata*,
but rather more authentic bolus grinders.
The mouth itself has undergone displacement.

Its effervescence, spent, brings up bouquets
of caries from the roots' fetidity,
seeped deep throughout the pelvic mandible.
It puts me, but reluctantly, in mind
of *nouveaux riches* just stumbled into town
from latifundia the size of countries,
with aspirations of urbanity.
By snickering Equestrians advised
to cultivate, with assiduity,
a fondness for the hint of "high corruption"
at table, such arrivistes hie to butchers
who educate them further in good taste
with pricey chitterlings, aged exquisitely.

An habitué, patrician, decadent,
of Palatine's *frou-frou* establishments,
with maxillary molars coddled, coaxed
to flake and wobble in his jaded head

(enamel sheared away, the quick exposed
to light of day, pulp sultrily athrob),
will savor what those serviceable stumps
can lend to, say, live baby nightingales
in piglets stuffed, slow-seethed with porpoise milk,
when, at the proper angle, he bites down.
From nerves that languish in the root canals
they loose, sauce-wise, a balanced modicum
of exudate, liquescent, sweet yet sour.

    Corruption wends, into the vital core,
its spiral way, where abstruse involutes
of relish take their disconcerting shape.
Then, up they open, cloying, citrusy,
yet with a sassy, brassy finish, due
to autolytic blends of ripened yeast—
but velvety, if one may say, robust.
Herbaceousness found paradoxical
in carnivore's incisors, such as Spado's,
gives foxy zest that needs eleven heartbeats
to register on connoisseurship's palate:
a reckoning of systole requisite,
each thump a ticking bite of agony,
that gnashes the most piquant spice of all,
in jolts from jaw to tongue to uvula
and back again. Just ask the better sort:
our Senators, who gladly gum the daggers
mad Nero flings in legislative sessions.

    Chomped down upon with vigor adequate,
a doomed bicuspid smacks like halitosis
now groaned from our dead boat's errant wreckage,
or sighs from 'shroom queens, on that wreck enthroned
ceramically. No ragout, roux nor gravy

reduced by woman's cookery competes
with flavors fermented on mossy mulch
or stewed in sloughs of hemorrhagic gums.

    On second thought, why must this broad aroma
be dental in its etiology?
It simmers from another category,
perhaps, of tissue, liquefied, necrotic,
and not Spado's vast pussy-tusks at all,
but membranes of red fizz that crackle, still,
upon the surface of that glut of weeds
and rags, that M-word-mumbling, off-putting
(and, incidentally, quite toothless) thing,
whatever it may be, not tapping now
but grabbing scapulae attached to me,
and mouthing in my ear intelligibly.

    In misery it gyrates. It says *ouch*
(or so I hear) again, and yet again:
monotony, unvaried indices
of heart's not being quite arrested yet;
inveterate pulsations, cruelly timed
to lull the sufferer to drowsiness.
(In semi-dreams your pain's personified,
thus lent deliberate malignancy.)
The lazy wavelets lap and clutch at me
till, unenthused, I slip a sidelong glance
to glimpse off-whiteness, hardened, just a tad,
amid the formlessness. Perhaps a rack
of ribs have shivered from a shattered sternum.

    The sight solicits autonomic gags,
not altogether displeasing. The 'shrooms
with hive-wine chaser wash my belly's bowl

then siphon to the tumbler of my head
by way of sinus passage. Servile blood
commixed with sundry ichthyosities
plus orts of late imperial abortion
make soup, from which I sip an apparition.

XVIII.

    I don't know if my ghoulish vision's cast
among my friend's dramatis personae,
his repertoire of wicked queens, mean momsies
and nihilistic slags (I hope not); but
the demoness I cling to, damned, deformed,
well known at Rome, is thought to haunt and stalk
the squalor that is rural Illyria:
contagion of the zone where we just breathed.

    Her torso doubles as her face, no head
on which to wedge a wig; and, terror to tell,
her nipples peer like eyes, umbilicus
a nose with snaggled nostrils ill-equipped,
the *orifícium úrethrae extérnum*
a mouth that all too readily descends
to vulgarism. If our transsexed priest
is now impersonating such a crass
provincialized grotesquerie as this—
instead of newborn-throttler Agrippina,
or Semirámis (rude to offshoot Jews),
or anti-familistical Medea,
or hip-strapped Messalina—I now grip
paired earlobes for salvation purposes,
where axillae should be.

                    Unsettling thought.
My chest inflates with aspirated spume
to know it's floating flush against the trunk
of an acephalic bugaboo. The witch
I thought we'd left behind, crownless, interred

so shallowly beneath Graptus's turf
(or, rather, muck) in astral form swims here.
Desirous of her shinglebob's return,
she gnaws my kneecap with a dunning chant
while cursing from castrato-crotch this cantus:

> *What derelict doer of ignorant labor,*
> *what slave-nephew rued by both auntie and mistress,*
> *what priestess's burden, what sorceress' barber,*
> *what bad-bargain drudger scalps biddies in distress?*

   Still further she twat-flatulates, to say,
"Who is the partial-birth boo-boo, the botched
mismanaged miscarriage, as dragged behind
his pushier sibling, grasping latter's heel,
preemptively undone before the doing,
his neck wrung by my inbuilt orca snatch?
Who resurrects from embryonic dead
to avenge with tardiness, with laggard's sloth,
with deficit of sweet solicitude,
with slipshod lackadaisiality
and—much as my heart weeps and breaks to say—
with laxness in the art of valeting?

   "What pseudo-servant disowns his possessor?
What bad boy does his very momsy in?
And who's Nero's fraternal twin?"

                              Cue Graptus.

XIX.

    Unpunctual, as typical in chattels
of his price range, he makes petite entrance.
Long-suffering (not much longer), he, upon
some minor sloshing of the random sea,
along with our brain fodder, has caught up.
(Predicted somewhat earlier, by me.)
Though not quite so defleshed as Spado said,
his ábdomen, already meager, now
near-skeletized, is the source of scarlet clouds
that cloak the semi-precious geometrics
of my hallucinated ocean floor.

    He does his best (substandard) to report
for duty, but can't muster wherewithal,
exhaling less than half a whisper, hoarse,
from what appears, before my honeyed eyes,
as lungs strained through a sieve of bone-chipped chaos.
The Illyrian's excuse (if there be one)
for dereliction of this grossest sort
is drowned out by his master's fretful fuss.

    Mistress, see me. I am here.
    I had trouble. Now I'm near.
    And I bring you—

    For lack of puff he can't achieve full period.

    Edematously buoyant is the Mistress,
and dwarfs us like the tall Symplégades.
She strikes a priestly pose, or priestessly,

her gaze on heaven fixed, where the She-God
of All Ineffability is not.
(The last I heard, she lounges in a grot—
but that requires terrain, when all we've got
is gas and liquid for a pious flaunt.)
I cannot say if Spado's unaware
of a party, third, approaching from the stern.
Acknowledgment's deliberately postponed,
perhaps, by way of torture, sly, prolonged,
much as a female parent might ignore,
for reasons, or for none, a tyke that whines
to play or shit or something. Easy enough
it would be to disdain, or feign disdaining,
from way up there, the thimble-splort and plash
of us grease spots upon this bottom plane.

> *Master, I did work today.*
> *No one beat or had to say.*

"It's too bad Crapped-Us couldn't spare the time
to join me," Spado lisps, preening herself
in sunbeams by her pretty bulk eclipsed
from our mere heads. "But here I am, embraced
within a sunlit womb, a weightless dream
of comfiness in balmiest of baths,
with porpoises to fetch me nice barrettes,
my bosom treated to exfoliation
by licking lampreys, tickling limpets, too,
a sea anemone bright'ning my navel.
My manservant would dazzle at my aspect,
until, with hints from me, he, gradually,
through thick Illyrian dimness, came to dread
this first leg of our katabasic fall,

berthless, unmoored, bereft of bearing, down
to featureless, untemperátured *death!"*

   At that last word the slave gives off a flinch.
It saps him, but he manages to squeeze
a recoil, more or less definable.
The billows get more lumpy, more opaque.
Not merely timorousness has been expressed.

   The only recognition of arrival,
the doubly unannounced upwash upon
our archipelago's exclusive shores,
is not of person (as it were), but object.
The óbese eunuch reaches down to poke
one pinky finger (nothing else will fit)
into the jar; then, prior to licking, finds
rhetorical excuse to sweep that digit,
adroitly, through our mutual atmosphere,
asperging Graptus (still unglanced-at) with
a clinging splash of cowslip-colored sweet.

   This might seem blessing, boon liturgical,
peculiar to practitioners of cults
devoted to quaint eastern deities.
But if, contrariwise, our priestess flings
with purpose, it's an act of cruelty.

   The wretch is wrung by flinches more defined,
of thicker opaque lumps his form is reft,
than by the *death*-word's exclamation point.
Illyrian at birth, thus reared in dirt,
his body's cursed and cowled with eczema
from bald spot down to corns on hammertoes.
This skin complaint must infiltrate, suffuse

his inchoate sensorium. The bare
suggesting of a single bee is torment,
productive of squirms, spasms, seeping weeps.
Their outright stings, however venomous,
would set his teeth (if he had some) on edge
far less than naked notions, simplest thoughts,
of bristles on their legs, their fuzzed abdómens,
on chronic rawness sprinkling pollen's itch.

    On all our troupe's adventures heretofore
he'd shudder off our luggage when in sight
of perviousness we hove: volcanic rocks;
or dried, split pomegranates under trees;
or she-toads hatching tadpoles from their backs.
Arrays of pin-pricks, dimples, vesicles
remind him of his own porosity,
since infancy a non-stop tribulation,
perpetual bait for tireless fingernails.

    "Ambrosia, bug-brewed" with which Spado,
in seeming inadvertence, plasters Graptus
is not unlike the potions, recondite,
our Princeps gives associates: a drink
of suicide, imperiously imposed—
sole difference being Nero's aconite,
contrarily, from inside out corrodes.
Coercion's just as blithe in either case.

    Our slaveling's more appalled to share a raft
with honey, oozing past that elm-sap seal,
than by what trauma ripped his own leakage,
less yellowish, more red.

Tom Bradley

                    Pathetic measure
of ardency to serve, be loved: he laid
bent hands upon our pot of irritant,
up-scrounged conveyance, floatful in a pinch,
and, like a mastiff mouthing a crazed duck,
dog-paddled terror Spado-ward. Graptus,
with every stroke, lived through a block of time
no more supportable than crucifees
must feel, who wait for legionnaires to break
their knees.

                And fascinating it would be
imagining how Adriatic salt,
sharp crystals in suspension, must abrade
the raw rim of the wound comprising him.

XX.

*Fetched your special sweeties, I
dove for them. I bring them by.*

To which, so far, forthcoming's no reply.

*Petrel flies on your left hand.
We can follow her to land.*

"He's saying something nautical, Spado."

"I hear and see myself, and maybe you.
Besides, it's obvious that any boy—"

*Mistress, don't ignore me. Soon
I'll be dead, but need a boon.*

"—who talks of birds and eggy auguries
in circumstances similar to these
is ignorant and silly. What a boy!
A lazy, tardy boy, who nothing knows
of navigation or, um, boat techniques.
Solidity is to his right, not left.
A landmass, perfectly serviceable,
is close enough that we true freeborn men,
whose ears aren't tamped with servile cérumen
and bits of scratchy beeswax, hear the grains
of beach frottáging, one against the next,
whenever salted wind scuffs up a ripple.
Is tardy-farty's head stopped up with pebbles?
Can't hear the jagged bits of broken shells

and rough grit clusters, pinkish coral silt
that, triturating yonder strand, must chafe?
Does foolish duty-shirker-boy not see
the skitter-crabs and urchins of the sea
whose tribadry will grate the shingle, scrub,
erode and pinch an earth-enwrapping rash
that neither dries nor smoothens, not so long
as, in the cosmos, sentience obtains?
What sort of flaky-drudgy-boy would coo
at birdies high up in the dust-blast sky
and fail to feel this palpability
down here on crumbly *terra nullius*,
where he's life-sentenced to an epidermis?
I'll tell you just what sort: a charter member,
in poorest standing, of the skinniest
Illyrian generation ever sold."

   Our corpulent castrato chooses now
to shift into her confidential mode,
which constitutes an eardrum-pounding "Shoosh"
and rumbling, rolling winks of boulder-eyes.

   "You must know, Aceronia," she whispers,
"this wraith would not admit it to himself,
but he believes his least constituent scurf
divine as the enthroned entirety
of our pot-bellied, deathless Emperor:
an equal, if you please, fraternal twin.
But nature, nurture, both collude to show
this clown, delusive self-aggrandizer,
by not so much as half a fleck possessed
of modishness accrued to Claudian *gens*
nor Julian tribal hoity-toity-poos.
So far from qualified to claim as kin

the high-tone Caesar Divi Filiùs
Augustus-blah-blah-blah, our yokel comes—"

"—from acorn scroungers. Yes, I know. Spado,
perhaps we ought to start—"

                        "By any chance,
might you be privy to the reason why
his graduating class of subsoil snouters
are more contemptible than their forebears?"

Blind Homer fits free gums with "ivory guards,"
set sturdily in double palisades
to fence in wooly speech till second thought
can comb its tail of indiscretion's burrs.
But I'm proved toothless as a yammering thrall,
reluctant to respond, yet without will
to curb a tongue that lurches like a ram.

"Now that you mention it," I bleat and lisp,
"a manuscript, uncopied, I once found
in Porticus Octaviae's high stacks,
purported from the pen of Elder Pliny,
expounds upon maneuvers, time gone by:
Dalmatian legions shifted to and fro,
barbarian lives disrupted."

                     Far be it
from me to pitch in on the loud bewailing
of cunctatory Graptus' lagged response
to Spado's want of pamp'ring. But no true
nor valiant Roman must demur to flaunt
arcana that, eavesdropping on Praetorians,

he's gleaned regarding our Imperium's
projections of will's impulse overseas:

> *Your slave must have undergone birth and poor nurture*
> *when General Fufius, Legatus Propraetor,*
> *went transadriatic and took up his tenure,*
> *Illyria his ladder to glories far greater.*
>
> *Skilled both as a soldier and market predictor,*
> *not mighty of stature, perhaps a tad lecherous,*
> *he yearned to head east and keep tabs, in particular,*
> *on swart-visaged Parthians, trousered and treacherous.*
>
> *By more than a cohort reducing the roster*
> *of conscripts who baby-sat Graptus and fellows,*
> *he stowed them and rowed them in small fleets of coasters*
> *to old Macedon, disembarking in shallows.*
>
> *Retracing Ovidius's route to stagnation,*
> *they trudge across Thrace and reship at Odessus*
> *to stir the black Euxine like Argonaut Jason,*
> *but drying oars sooner, at Pontic Trapézus.*
>
> *Armenian satraps are bribed to say nothing*
> *as Fufius peeks at the dregs of the Persians*
> *in Mesopotamian shit-pits galumphing*
> *on overgrown horses, inspiring aversion.*
>
> *To compensate legionnaires left in the garrison,*
> *brave spearmen short-handed by one or two regiments,*
> *the Gen'ral tells slave-traders, "Cull those Illyrians!"*
> *Rome's auction blocks stack up with substandard specimens.*

"Correct. Yes. Fine. I got it," Spado huffs.
(He seems to've known the answer all along.)
"Forgive me. Are you finished? May I speak?"

"There's something else, appalling, apropos,
about this Fufius, appertaining to
great-aunties and gorgons—"

                                                  "Another time."

XXI.

Dove for sweeties. I dove well.
Something fought me. Down there still.

Need to go away. We do.
Master, I'm so scared for you.

"I've let you narrate Grabbed-Ass in tykehood,
a vendible price unit fetched to town
as minor plugger-up of market glut.
Yourself have witnessed, recently, firsthand,
his fond homeland return, when he re-sailed
this sea, attendant on our expedition,
to have a hand acquiring my hairpiece.
Aceronia, dear, of that you're well informed.
Am I correct?"

"No. Please. I really can't—"

"Or maybe not? I seem to recollect
a certain waiting-lady, like a foetus,
curled, cringing tight, among the tendrils, twigs
and partly gummed acorn cupules. Your eyes,
though 'shroomed, were useful, yes? Lack of response
I'll take as maybe.

"The old sorceress,
uncivilized, would preen herself to be
a priestess, as it were, rival to me.
(Positions more secure aren't hard to find.)
And in her sacerdotish fakery

the conjure-biddy proved more disinclined
to unclaw jars of fungal sacrament
than render up her freckled pate.

                                "In spite
of her presumptive esoteric skills,
she wound up seeming, more or less, to die.
That goes unsaid, d'you think? Can one survive
sans padding on the seams where head bones mesh?"

"The Elder Pliny nowhere treats of such—"

"Her nephew is the one to ask."

                                    "How so?"

"As you, my dear, in wet black ventricles
of your unspoken brain, can't but suspect,
the prank was his idea. None of mine!"

   The óbese eunuch pauses now for something—
what, I can't say—that shifts in my affect.

"Those slinking house cats inexplicably
maintained by certain un-Romans as pets
will bring bits of their mousy prey to Mistress,
as worshipful tribute. Can she refuse,
without a catastrophic consequence,
like goddesses displeased by roasted thighs
upon a fleece-strewn beach, botched holocausts,
who send forth tidal waves to make meat broth?
Humanity attributes to Minerva
her butch helmet; so Graptus upon me
has set this gorgon aegis, ribboned, blond—

but first the little savage had to latch
his pincers on.

    "And wonder you well might,
Aceronia—my love, my number-one,
my favorite member of my entourage,
whom I esteem so infinitely higher
than any mere Illyrian, unfree,
with bad complexion—how a bug physique
like Graptus's could flay a witchy skull.
Let me assure you, he got well behind it,
up to the crackly wrists. Imagine that,
his own tribeswoman. What disloyalty!
Self-hating much? Oh, Aceronia, please!
His sweet great-auntie! But, throughout the chore,
of course, he whinged, as much from accidie
as feigned distaste, for no more shiftless slave,
nor indolent, has ever been abducted
as rickety urchin by myopic merchant
from sadness-drooping sloughs of moss and mold
and fetched across the Adriatic, cold,
in leaky ship, to be got rid of, cheap,
cut-rate, on-special, in Transtibertine.

 "The lad's not here to plead his case, it's true;
and one must not talk nasties 'bout the *dead*—"

 Another tortured flinch is roundly wrung
by that D-word from Graptus' luckless trunk,
accompanied by further reddish lump
release, along with extra anguished moans.

 "—but collared critters have no right of self
(nor any other) -défense, anyway."

Just barely audible to anxious me,
by eunuch's ears ignored elaborately,
Graptus' accounting for his acts and being
come groaning through the chunks of foam and slave:

> *I saw Gr'Auntie's teats stare out.*
> *Belly-button turned to snout.*
> *Lady-hole bit like a mouth.*
>
> *Teeth and tongue I felt down there.*
> *Mistress, we must not stay here.*

Not precisely in response, but once again
in his true countertenor, Spado speaks,
and looks into my eyes. (To tell the truth,
I much prefer his self's alternatives.
The female figures from our mythic past
are not so unrelievedly unkind.)

"Indeed, yes: 'Gr'Auntie'—or some other class
of dickless forebear. Quite impossible
to narrow down much further than generic
with unregenerate Transadriatics.
They've not invented family yet, nor wedlock,
and, unsuspicious of their babies' source,
assume the latter spring spontaneously
through acts of will on slaggy slatterns' part,
who by the litter defectate wet broods,
each semi-solid preemie snaggled worse
than elder siblings, on whose brittle heels
it follows, pooped in ever-thinning layers
on clammy, weird, forlorn Illyrian mud."

Terror teeth in crushing pairs.
I took more than Gr'Auntie's hair.

Master, I can't be dead yet.
Something Graptus needs to get.

The warning and the importune are heard
by no castrati in the neighborhood,
and only just perceived by me, for lack
of volume adequate to top Spado.
The Master's meanwhile swelled to mannish mode,
effeminacy's lingering lisp expunged
again, in favor of bull sentiment,
up-belched, and virtue, gruff but clement, which
the óbese eunuch, when she's feeling bored
or cruel (all day today, so far), employs
to praise her dead slave in absentia.

"Stout laddy-buck, our Graptus, all in all,"
snorts Spado.

Too pathetic's the effect.
The dying thrall forgets the boon he craves,
along with any entrails presently
he might be sending to the sandy floor
(those into piscine gullets undetoured),
and physically gets buoyed, three fingers' width,
from his own gore-slick. Momentarily,
he has his own castrato carved from cork
for clinging to.

"You bet!" the Mistress booms
with just sufficient masculinity
to thrill, and nearly kill, her manservant.

"The rascal-scamp did pretty darn okay
outfitting the old boss with this toupée.
A snug fit. Sporty. Suction stood up good
to that dad-blasted shipwreck, well withstood.
It stayed screwed tight on this thick-bristled knob
o' mine. My boy's so rig'rous as to've tanned
that critter's frizzy fell in caustic blends
of tough ingredients, plunged both bare hands—"

"Please, Spado, spare me. I don't need to know."

That interruption, which I might have shrieked,
gives him a start, or her, just jolt enough
to shunt our gelding out of Daddy mode
and back to "dicklessness." Where he left off
is where she re-begins:

               "—in potion, hot,
compounded of the ex-proprietor's
substantia grisea, minced and blent
with first-in-morning castrato wee-wee,
from guess who's chatty meàtus—tee hee!
And don't forget the secret spice, from dogs."

"No, really? Dogs?"

               "That's right."

                     "King Eumenes
of Pergamum, in days gone by, patron
of clever Greeklings, spurred them to invent
a fabulous material with that 'spice'—"

"You don't say," mutters Spado. "Don't tell me.
You're getting this from Elder—"

                              "Leftovers,
inedible, from banquets, hecatombs,
she-goat- and ox- and sheepskins, were of fat
well-scraped, the split hides soaked in special brews
with carefully selected 'spices'—"

                                     "Turds."

"—from purebred mastiffs."

                                     "Key ingredient."

Elaborate alchemy's pulled by those Grecians.
(Eumenes insists on the recipe's encryption.)
Voilà! Parchment's born with all charming discretion.
And now we have books without troubling Ægyptians!

"Not much a reader, me," the castrate yawns.

It's slightly less dear than papyrus, sole medium
for which it competes 'mongst our scribblesome fellows.
A week's wage for freemen who're paid for their tedium
is still plenty pricey: one drachma per folio.

Your non-splinter Jews use the same basic formulae
to publish their Asian-style Iliads, Odysseys,
Aeneids and Batrachomyomachiae,
but throw pious kinks in the tanning processes.

The coveted fruits of their Judean date trees,
whose sweetness brings weight-for-weight trading in silver,

*replace in the brew taboo animal feces,
and thus pursue Hebrews their bent as lawgivers.*

"In Graptus' homeland, nothing grows that's sweet,
and nothing worth a thousandth part its weight
in grossly alloyed tin, much less pure argent.
That's given, as you know, Spado, too well.
But how, in in this or any other world,
could he have mastered dog shit's subtleties?"

"I've no idea where my—let's be frank—
enfeebled household minion got that lore,
transmitted orally among, perhaps,
the headhunters of weird Illyria.
Acquired by hearsay, brought in secondhand
by some Aeolian cordwainer's butt-boy,
repatriated after manumission,
who yammered—"

        "Wait a moment. Headhunters?"

"The cult Great-Auntie-poo officiates.
Whence else would dawdling primitives derive
prodigious surgical proclivities?"

"Illyria's just across—"

        "I know, I know.
Appalling, isn't it?"

        Spado adjusts
the ribbons on his "aegis," whispering this—

"Do any empires spring to mind, my dear,
that, thinly spread administratively,
could stand a modicum, if just a pinch,
of cheekie-tightening? I won't name names;
but this is ludicrous, am I not right?
Are noggins burgled just across the ditch?
Some brigandage and pirates, if a smidge,
are well enough, and good; but, honestly,
another sordid matter altogether
is local 'culture,' this indigenous
malignancy of marrow. It requires
expungement forthwith. Immemorial
traditions must be rinsed away with baths,
with aqueducts, with travertine façades,
cute mini-fora, quaintly wrapped togas
and smears of limewash."

                        One such indigene,
a bit too fond of cranial venery,
in our immediate vicinity,
now tightens his own "cheekies," as it were,
and generates from naught sufficient wind
to speak, with puff for ten words, not one more.
The first, especially, can't be ignored—

    Manumission's boon I crave.
    Master, I can't die a slave.

XXII.

    Medusa's head swings by reptilian braids
that cinch about the bright-pigmented fist
of Perseus, sea monster-petrifier,
her face a revelation in egg tempera
of every horror that jabs into or screams
out from the eye: uncanny evidence
of famous Grecian Cydias's brush
upon a terracotta slab, once found,
quite inexplicably, among the beads
and fetishes devoted to a god,
Armenian Jove (real name unknown to me),
in temple precincts roundly desecrated,
the votives looted (gorgon's portrait, too)
by aforementioned General Fufius
returning home from Parthian reconnoiters.

    For a million silver sésterces (enough
to buy one Senate seat) old Fufius sells
the sleep-exterminating masterpiece
to one of Rome's more gauzy, wealthy pathics,
who, far from finding Snaky-Locks "off-putting,"
installs her in his swank *triclinium*
to edify some posh patrician chums
at the social season's most exquisite fête.

    However screened for exclusivity,
the banquet's infiltrated by a plebe
in borrowed toga, maladroitly wound
about his unheroic frame. His tongue
(that is to say, my tongue), as always glib

when under pressure, talks me past the gate
along with my grim curiosity.

   Rome's finest, pedigreed impeccably,
their blood to Latium brought on nameless ships
in ancient days, by feathered Nubians
palanquinned up the Palatine, perfect
exemplars of manhood, my fellow guests
recoil in terror from the dining room
where Gr'Auntie hovers o'er the laden tables.
Regrouping in the *peristylium*,
they tremble into goblets, talk of races,
of politics, of anything but art,
there driven by the sheerness of the hate
that's screaming from the monstress' ochre eyes.

   More trepidated even than my betters,
not brave, rather insatiably morbid
(a quality to stand me in good stead
as charter member of the eunuch's troupe),
in the banquet hall, alone, I cower, swoon
before Phorcys's daughter, stare her down,
though slowly being aged by the bare sight—
by *her* sight, rather, perforating me:
Graptusian trypophobic honeycombs.
A paralytic period I abide,
the meantime making small hiccoughing sounds,
until the German butler (natural blond,
a savage scared by no mere tinted daubs)
ejects me from the house.

                    And yet, today,
if I could swim but half a stroke, I'd froth
the panicked Adriatic with retreat

from Spado's face. The terracotta snarl
was like a flute girl's flirty glance compared
to what burns over me. More baneful blast
of ire with trace of rational restraint
unmixed, I've never seen. The demoness
no longer's acephalic. She has grown
a spheroid on her shoulders just to house
two orbs that might be called celestial
in magnitude, if not for hellish cast.
Miraculously, the object of that hate
has not to steam spontaneously sublimed.

   The óbese eunuch's looking, finally,
upon her hemorrháging slave.

                         "What did
you just say?"

           Manumit me, Mistress, please—

   Uprisen arm, the left one, lurching high,
a sperm whale's mile-long flipper's fixed to deal
that single downward swipe, that "gizzard chop,"
with which to "re-kill": guaranteed death-blow
athwart the filaments that loosely loop
a life (so-called) to Graptus.

                       Our doldrum's
subséquent tidal wave is in the offing.
I've time to hug the hate-transcending cruse
of fungal kindness, tolerance, charity
against my all-too-bony torso; squeeze
its elm sap shut; wince, too, my head's inlets.

    Before your queen can strike, the Adriatic
we've come to know and not entirely rue
as terminal predicament, jiggles
like aspic once again, and vanishes,
this time without preserving weightlessness.
The hypo-panorama, unparqueted,
moves closer than its wonted several miles.
We're smitten, yes, but not from overhead.

    One's legs, accustomed to passivity,
get useless under sudden birthing's bulk.
One's jaw is kneed by doubled knockout blows.

XXIII.

    I find myself cross-legged, buttocks slammed
on something like a beach: a flaky patch
of Spado's "earth-enwrapping rash." I nurse
what Graptus called, in slavish trochee-grunt,
our "special sweeties." Honey-glued to me,
the jar has formed a less than perfect seal
on my ribs' corrugations, ill-equipped,
contemptibly, with no salvation-grips.
Contamination's what I fear, and all
I think of: salt's adulterating seep
overcomplexifying 'shroom bouquet.

    In a reddened tidal puddle just next door
is spasming Graptus. Mistress squats and holds
her dying slave as though already dead,
while striking poses, as per usual.
From her impersonation repertoire,
this time, Geb's daughter, Isis, gets the part.
She's grieving for her husband, defunct son,
or both, whichever. (These Ægyptians
aren't easy to interpret.)

                    "So, my boy,"
the eunuch yawns, while shaking dunes of grit
from her bouffant, ensuring plenteous grains
are peppering the membranes that, exposed,
lie mucously aquiver in her lap.
"How are you holding up? Do let me know.
In *very* general terms."

"You're kind to ask,
dear Mistress, mine," the whisper comes, no less
than previously moribund, but lent
lucidity by touch of Priestess-Momsy,
Antaeus-like (not quite so butch). "I've felt
much better in the past. But please don't fret
for merely me."

              He tries to, but cannot
refrain from coughing something tubular,
approximately solid, blackish-red,
a web of whitish gristle at one end.

"Contain yourself!"

                    The castrate winks at me,
brimmed with self-fondness for her drollery.

"You always offered, Master, to reveal
my origins to me, someday, before
I pass into the Afterworld. I fear
today's the day, or else a promise breached."

"The *After*world, of course!"

                    In my direction
the óbese eunuch casts mischievous smirks.
His mouth side-murmurs, so the dupe won't hear—

"What do the splinter-Jews, those ingrates, say
when pseudo-Semirámis buys their boys,
redeeming little ones from mastiffs' jaws?
Something about millstones for necklaces
and going for a swim? Both chic and fun!"

    Some superficial words, but dutiful,
descend to Spado's lap:

            "Be comforted,
if necessary, Crapped-Us, by the doctrine
which I, your catechist, have fed you true:
our Goddess Most Ineffable will greet,
with sympathy, with soft solicitude,
the weary, weak, downtrodden, measly, meek
foregathered in the—"

            Spado barely tries
suppressing catty snickers as he coos
the next word:

        "—*Afterworld.*"

                It's followed up
with jolly elbows, joshing the poor wretch
in gnawed-off sinking ribs, eliciting
a sigh of grim mortality—or just
a bubbling puff from pulmonary punctures.

    Above burst belly, Spado rolls his eyes
facetiously at Aceronia,
who's wondering if her lady-skull can hold
another fist-to-mouth of fungus—not
surfeited by red caps with bright white spots
so much as honey, endless, crystallized
against the rear walls of her eyeballs.

                    "Who
obliged herself to narrate your beginnings?
You're sure the twat who promised that was me?"

"Not 'twat,' but, yes. You said before I died."

"Well, bless this Grand Imperatrix's sweet,
hot cicatrix if I don't misrecall
the undertaking of that brittle vow."

"Perhaps you'd better tell me true today."

"Nonsense, my laddy-buck, never so stout!
One doesn't really need these reddish-blacks,
these sausages and wads, rim-spilling out
in gay profusion from your, um, thorax.
In no time you'll be plenty fit to scout
damp firewood, fetch us cloying berries, nuts,
and mutilate with vigor any sum
of helpless, elderly close relatives."

But then the eunuch comes to realize
death's-door denial, disingenuous,
deprives the Mundus of a marvelous
theatrical display. Geldings must clutch
such moments bittersweet, poignant, as these.
Unfamilied existence, like our Spado's,
precludes unfaked scenes of maudlinity
between linked, or just glued-together, souls.
Therefore, with due dispatch, he changes roles
before the chance can pass—or pass away.

"Allow me," says my traveling companion,
"to get more comfortable."

                        Her dimply thighs
are to an attitude more motherly
and mournful jostled, like a bas-relief

of Horus' momsy cradling that defunct
propinquity. This posture, fully stiff
and hieratic, being fom the Nile,
and not intended to accommodate
unmummified yet traumatized remains,
elicits a release of further entrails,
and would have wrenched a scream of pure distress,
if Graptus, languishing, possessed the puff.

   Pondering awhile the tiny spectacle
(see how Illyrians fade so readily!),
in mild-ish irritation Spado sighs
and says, magnanimously, "I suppose,
in circumstances déclassé as these,
I'm comfy as I'll ever likely get.
So now I'll tell your origins to you."

   Hung dangling halfway off the abysmal rim
recalled by no one at first hand, Graptus,
reluctant drudger, toils and hauls himself,
one finger's width, back; tries to open up
the slave entire, not merely ears, nose, eyes
and ventral cavity, but spirit, too:
that Strange Invisible, which, he assumes,
remains inside him still, as yet unspilled.
His Master, priest of the Ineffable
She-God, has taught him never to deny
that airy inner-bugaboo's strict fact
nor eternality. Such sweet faith lends
amenability to nonstop work
while stitched inside a sack, disposable,
of slave-skin here and now, soon shed and left.

Great-Auntie's nephew, like a wound fresh-slashed
or oyster popped with gases, gaping, craves
the boon of knowledge: salty facets rubbed
into his mind's skin rash; intelligence
he's itched to scratch since comprehending speech.
Avidity for long-term promise kept,
bestowing smidgens of biography,
alone prolongs this one last grind, called "life,"
about to drain into the sand.

      "If you
don't calm down, boy, sit still and stop your slosh
of unshat shit on my venereal *mons*,
I won't reveal a blessed thing," scolds Momsy,
who's on the verge of getting pettish, pouty.
Castrati tend to slap when in that mood,
as we've been told.

    "I'm sorry, Mistress! Please,
for all Ineffability's sweet sake,
don't punch me!"

    Agrippina takes a breath
to self-compose. Her eyes commence to roam,
with mine, the ground on which our touring troupe's
upwashed. Which path, by animal desire
pre-beaten, shall we, anabasis-wise
(once duly's been discharged this cheerless chore,
quasi-Homeric seashore exequy),
bestir ourselves to clamber?

      Quietly
(to spare any valets, big-eared, who might
be craving boons in the vicinity

and hoping not to die or be abandoned
before said boons are graciously indulged),
through corners of our eyes, we free men scope
for gaps in yonder dry geology
that might lend furtherance to odysseys—
if that grand term, without inspiring jeers,
is not too strictly inapplicable
to such propulsiveness as we've displayed.

   At present Sol Invictus still has not
stopped laying down his trail of snail-gray snot
across the featurelessness of the vault.
He's going down like an Athenian
on one of our Proconsuls.

                       I hear me,
as through another's throat, officiously—

   "Before things get all crawly, quaint and dark,
it might behoove us to attain that rise
and get our bearings, if they're gettable
without unduly inconveniencing
a certain, as it were, scout—"

                    "Shhh! Someone's
having herself a Moment, in *quadrata*."

   The eunuch, indicating *you-know-who*
with muted downward glances at the mass
across his thighs slopped so affectingly,
now looks around a bit, shudders and says—

   "Such a peculiar place. The seashells come
in way too many colors."

Tom Bradley

            "Just what I
was going to say."

            Our priest begins to rock,
first back, then forth; hip-twists tossed in, a few.
Though histrionically they're justified,
these motions cause his chattel to contort
in what, with any luck, is not the pain,
the unimpeded kind, that can, I've heard,
induce insanity.

            The Dowager
in rhythm croons lullabiography:

> *Your momsy was addled, her fur red like ochre*
> *and bestial, so Fufius decreed her perditiom*
> *'mongst offerings-up to the belly-faced ogre*
> *who gnaws pregnant victims in your quaint tradition.*
>
> *And, just as they brained her with one of the pebbles*
> *your people call "implements," out Graptus gushes*
> *(and not from her skull; don't self-flatter): a devil*
> *to cast outside "walls," as your tribesmen name bushes.*
>
> *Exposed to the "elements" (as locals term drizzle)*
> *upon a turd-pile, euphemized as a "peat bog,"*
> *tripped on by a trafficker draining his pizzle,*
> *collected, you're tucked next to lunch in his kit bag.*
>
> *This entrepreneurial spirit, who's hawking*
> *what no one calls "humans," unscrupuled to bother*
> *to deal in untainted goods, drags you to auction*
> *and somehow unloads you on my own, er, mother—*

(My friend urps, gags and all but barfs upon
bare mention of that second loaded M-word.
It might be interesting to bring, someday,
the transsexed creature out upon this topic—
perhaps inland, when my own gut's un-queased.)

*—who must've been drunk. Brand-new pet in our household,
your life's consecrated to whimsies and cruel ploys,
not bright, but possessed of impressive pain thresholds,
my valet and plaything and, frankly, my butt-boy—*

*—that is, till, with sharp shard and piety brimming,
my solemn ordination in priesthood's strict regimen.
And then you got bitten by something while swimming:
a fish or an aunt. Origins? There, you've heard them.*

The look on Graptus' undersized phiz shows
not shock, dismay nor disbelief so much
as disappointment—but a letting-down
accustomed, so inveterate as to cause
no change. As easily might rhapsodies,
all hymning dim divinity, with hints
of, several generations back in time,
a problematic drip of Claudian *gens*
and Julian tribe, been trilled in Spadic lisps,
or rumors of bored dalliances, gang rape
by more or less Italian legionnaires,
the unrelieved Illyrianness hybridized.

So what? It's still another sack to fill,
a pot to be outpoured, a further mess
that needs the hefting-up to Mistress' lips,
the intercepting at her other end.

Graptus can barely mouth his gratitude
for this metempsychotic insight.

                        "Thank
you, Master."

        "You are welcome—"

                    Spado waits
a half a heartbeat.

        "—birthday-boy!"

                    Those words
send shudders up the ruined corpus. Pain,
concomitant, brings to the thrall's spent mind
a certain sharpness, without precedent.
He's able to respond at normal volume,
almost.

    "Today's my—?"

            "What did I just say?"

  "So I'm of age! I'm finally fit to render
my gender to the She-God!"

                  "Oh, that's right!
How could old Agrippina have forgot?
You're in a tight predicament, are you not?
Gracious! Your future in the *After*world
is hanging in the balance—or, rather,
slung in your scrotal sac."

          "Please, Mistress, dear,
my guide into the Realm Ineffable,
your Graptus' hands are lacking implements,
his arms the strength. While yet lifetime remains,
select a colored, sharp and shattered shell.
Deballock me!"

          "Oooh, no!" the gelding shrieks,
and shoves the pious postulant away.
It turns out necessary, several times,
to scrape and scoop each glop of ardency
and clot of genuine vocation off
old Momsy's lap. Graptus's eczema
with grit and granules, at the puddled feet,
gets coated, while his boss screeches—

          "She-God
amerce and mulct you till the Mundus fizzles!
Distasteful pecker-snot! How dare you blab
about your private parts at such a time,
when Agrippina squats uncomfortably?
Besides, if you don't mind my asking much,
d'you see, within an easeful forearm's reach,
a chip of sea-scab, suitably serrated?"

   "So crush that cruse, cradled protectively
against the breasts of her, your favored love,
your special pet within our touring troupe,
and, in the manner Anatolian,
sublimely orthodox, made true by time,
employ a shard to consecrate me now."

   "Oooh, no!" both free girls shriek in unison.
With teats I shield our stash of honey-smooch.

"Don't make me do what Larissan beavers do."

I look up, puzzled, from the 'shrooms and ask
the Master, "What in Dis Pater's dread name
and Nero's, too, is that supposed to mean?"

"You do not want to know."

                        "I do," I say,
and Spado tells me.

          "Then," weeps Graptus, "please
honor your other promise, that I die
in manumission."

          That M-word, the third,
comes off, this time, no happier than before.
Again the sperm whale's mile-long flipper hoists
on high: no threat of inundation now,
but temblors, Neapolitan-style.

                     But then
something—don't ask me what—stays Spado's limb.
Arrested is his homicidal bent,
or sublimated temporarily.
Like elephant proboscises, tendons
and arteries come swollen in his throat
as, with no minor effort, he refrains
from punching and belaboring the lad
(a mess no less than murder, were it done).
Methodically, through moderated tusks,
the óbese eunuch to his hemorrhaging slave
delivers calm harangue:

"If you'd but pay
attention to somewhat or someone else
besides your genitalic whimsies, boy,
if you'd but flex neck ligaments to raise
your stunted knob up from my thighs and swivel,
no more than just a bit, before the sun
abandons, finally, his naïve urge
to lighten these procedures on my beach,
perhaps you'd notice, Grabbed-Ass, that we've breached
uncharted territory. Do you see
baths, aqueducts and travertine façades,
cute mini-fora trolled by gauzy pathics
with droopy recta? Tell me, do you see
municipality or magistrate?
Where is, pray tell, the legal apparatus
to effect this complex transaction you crave,
this manumission?

"And, in any case,
I don't suppose you've troubled to bestir
yourself, across the many dragging decades
of our association, here and there,
a copper to secrete, accumulate,
through steady thrift and industry, your due
peculium, by which, with honesty,
might purchased be that boon you coyly beg
as loose gratuity from me. D'you expect
your Mistress to take up such sleazeful slack?
Yes? Here we have unfree morality,
so typical of drudgers. Can you grasp
the grotesquerie of your presumptuousness?
Aren't you ashamed?"

             "But ever since before
I'm able recall, I've slaved. It's time—"

   "I do not seem, just now, to have, Crapped-Us,
the means to pay your liberation tax
right handy."

          Moments, supercilious,
are spent hefting an absent purse, fish-chewed,
and to the greedy sea floor long since sunk.

   "And what is five percent of your fair price?
May I assume you've reckoned up the sum,
all calculated, pinched and bundled, tucked
about your person, or what's left of latter,
coins wedged betwixt the discs of your flayed spine?
Do I recall, once, with benevolence,
before you grew (and so halfheartedly)
out of a toddler's tresses, teaching you
your by-the-hundreds in avoirdupois,
sesterces, too? You surely have retained
that lesson—or do I presume? Pop quiz!
What's thirteen times six forty-eighths—"

                              I hear
somebody shout (it turns out to be me),
"Whoah! Spado!"

          The possessor of that most
peculiar moniker is startled, stopped.
From where she squats in next door's ebbing pool
(increasingly tinctured a thickish red)
she squints across into my honeyed voids,

where something, possibly, can be descried
resembling emotion.

      "What?" he says,
and checks himself for pendent nasal dirt.

 "A little, um—"

      I pause to belch mushrooms
into the basement of my soft palate,
where they impart Chrestiani wisdom.

          "—um,
a little fellow-feeling might be felt
in certain situations. Don't you think?"
Sort of?"

    "Fellow—?"

      In unfeigned puzzlement
the óbese eunuch's exponential face
appears as, years ago, it might have done
before the multiplicities of shams
and interlocking self-deceits accrued,
just prior to squawking self-announcement, when
his fontanelle, placenta-cowled, squeezed past
his own M-word's neglectful quim-sphincter.

 "I've no idea what you're on about.
A certain waiting-lady would do well
to ease off gobbling untreed ears, breathe deep
and, rather than with weird non-sequiturs
disrupting these sad obsequies, perhaps
condole with me on my bereavement, me,

who nearly reared this dim defunctitude.
You have been chastised, Aceronia.

"So, anyway, where were we, laddy-buck?
Here I sit, a-prattling with your rival
in Empress Dowager's affections, when
it's your great-biggish special hoo-ray Moment.
How I go on, old biddy me, scarce fit
for niching 'midst Rome's pantheon! So, what
is on your, so to speak, as it were, 'mind'?"

The dying thrall no sooner unpries jaws
than's interrupted, balked—

                    "'Fellow-feeling'?"
The eunuch turns again to me. "Don't saints,
heroical and Stoical, like you,
go flitting 'round preaching contempt for death?
Well, look around you, Seneca. Just who's
the most contemptible of our fun trio?
Fellow-*fellatio*'s more like it.

                "Oh,
I'm sorry, boy. I couldn't but refute
your baby sister's point with rhetoric,
that devastating tool of momsy minds.
You've just witnessed, lucky Illyrian,
deployment of Greekling philosophy.
It's left the slut quite speechless, sans rebuttal,
undemurely moping 'round in yonder grit,
all petulant. Please do continue with—
whatever."

Tom Bradley

        "Do not let me die a slave."

   "Oh, yes. That's right. The manumission thing.
From your unhappy affect I discern—
or, rather, from your chronic sullenness—
that you, Graptus, consider me to be
in some moral arrears to you, vaguely
expecting me to conjure priestess-craft
and make the boo-boo that is you all better.
You hope to be my freedman, then my client.
In that capacity, no doubt, you'll claim
right of appeal to the Imperator
next time my whim's to have you crucified."

   With effortless disdain available
to Empresses exclusively, Spado
remarks aside to me—

        "It mystifies,
but menial types do love to breathe, so much,
they'd rather dwindle twenty, thirty years,
legs shackled to the damp mephitic stones
of Caesar's overcrowded holding cells,
awaiting the foregone adjudication
of hopelss fantasies they call 'reversals,'
than grab the chance a makeshift gibbet's stretch
affords right-thinking slaves. I've always told
this scamp, this scatterbrained man-baby-boy,
dark birds immediately consume his eyes
with mercy, sparing him the spectacle
of self's dismantlement, tacked on that tree.
Am I correct, or not, Lady-in-Waiting?
Feel free to share your feelings."

                        Elder Pliny
discusses crows and crucifixions, but,
at this point neither can I bring to mind,
nor are my tongue and teeth equipped to cite
book, chapter, verse. I seem to be inspecting
this jar for cracks, this honey for seepage.

  "White salt," instead, I hear me trumpeting,
"might just enhance our red love's potency!"

  "I see. Well, thank you for that insight, dear.
Graptus, my rodent freedman, I suppose
you'll want to adopt my *nomen,* way down deep
inside the Underworld, expecting me
to take it as a compli—"

                "*Underworld?*"

XXIV.

    In strictest acceptation of the verb,
is Spado savoring the new expression
that bleeds so suddenly from Graptus' face,
or wilfully ignoring this fresh grimace,
this unfamiliar reconfiguration
of tiny features, heretofore content
with stupors, winces, raptures, numb despair
but, till now, never torqued in abject horror?

    "But, Master, the Goddess Ineffable
has reassured us that—"

                          At all events,
for sake of while's beguilement, our priestess,
though consecrated to the ministry
of Anatolia's mother cult, proceeds
to pooh-pooh that salvationistic creed,
upon whose tenets, milky, fatuous,
she's caused her dupe to drape a lifetime's hopes,
from beardlessness until this crisis.

                                But
in order that complete annihilation
should be achieved in Graptus' heart, and give
herself the maximum—shall I say "joy"?—
our cruel castrato first must condescend
to gather back eczematousness up
from endless itching powders of the strand
on which the thrall's summarily been scooped,
and to resume the stylized mourning pose,

authentically Isiac. (It were better,
I can affirm, for the integrity,
already feeble, of the skeleton,
so few connective tissues still unfrayed,
to leave it on the ground.)

                Disburdening
the boy of all belief commences so:

  "When crowing that you'll soon be fit to fetch
us berries, wood and extra blond headgear,
exaggeration was indulged, I fear.
Mendacity's a stretch for us castrati,
reluctant to unmake our made-up selves.
So you'll be fed no further falsity.
Your Agrippina, having birthed your being,
owes truth, Graptus, to you, with fewer smirks.

  "Let's start with frank appraisal, unflinching,
of your condition (physical, that is)
as, understandably, you won't look down
to estimate your own catastrophe:

> Your belly's indented with scallops and pinkings.
> Serrated teeth sunken, sloughed off in your breastbone
> (hold still; ivory triangles, pretty!—stop blinking!),
> lead me to deduce, boy, that you have been chewed on.
>
> For 'xample, have ghosts of smooth-domed conjure-ladies
> condensed from the fog of Illyrian boneyards
> and gnawed you, conjoined with sororal twin babies
> who strut strange deformities—what's that Greek loan-word?

"Acephaly," is my reply. "Not like
these bonbons. Tiny Chresti, they sport caps
of red with pretty spots of sinless white.
To these heads will my unscalped soul be doffed.
Vagina déntata's beside the point."

> *Of course, dear, thank you. I blame dolphins, who drip with*
> *the sputum of Neptune. Ungainly, abusive,*
> *they never come headless, but standard-equipped with*
> *those hardly attractive sincipital pussies.*

Having propounded that hypothesis,
complacently the eunuch turns to me,
parenthesizing—

"Aceronia, see?
The point's not jeering in the face, merely,
of organisms' slow decrepitude,
but probing guts' esthetic subtleties
while yet the precious chance remains to delve.
Watch this—"

Not gingerly enough to suit
the patient, foot-long fingers romp and grope.

"Just as I feared. I'm palpating no shred,
nor flake, nor furfuraceous sliver, nor
a half-dandruff of doubt. You're dying, Graptus:
my diagnosis and my gnosis, both.
I oversold the disutility
of these slick tubes, this spillage, puckering,
aromatizing in our parching puddle.
You can't be counter-baptized like your sibling,
since we're delivered from the sacral fluid.

In my high quality as your advisor,
initiatrix into mysteries,
I might suggest you thrice expectorate
into your bosom, gaining She-God's grace
as per the Anatolian usage. But—"

A gesturing palm cups through concavity.

"—you have nowhere ligurgically to spit.
Not only are you shedding this cracked shell
(to shift such shambles lucky, anyhow,
which has to hurt)—"

She pokes around some more.

"—but verging on awareness-loss, forever."

It's plain that proposition sits unwell
with Graptus, flimsy though his jeopardized
awareness be.

Shortage, atypical
(and surely feigned), of words makes Agrippina
but briefly grab the air and wave about,
to sift for sounds that suit her sense's needs—

"Boned-up on doctrines our Ineffable
reveals anent the immortality,
salvageability, as well, of souls—"

She eyes the seascape, recently vacated,
with wistfulness.

"—and cognizant of this
being neither best of times nor perfect place
to moot the skeptic's qualms—"

                                            She blushes pink
and simpers, self-charmed by her girlish lack
of bedside manners and (if words aren't minced)
funereal decorum.

                         "—even I,
a priestess, such as you hankered, as well,
in masturbátory dreams, one day to be,
and never will (not due to lack of class;
salvation cults are tolerant that way;
the difficulty's, rather, scheduling,
you fast-expiring, failed, sad supplicant)—
yes, even an initiate adept
of full-blown mysteries, like me, your momsy,
meets doubtful moments (dead incredible
as that might sound) when our sublime belief's
all-loving consolation, plank of hope,
will shiver, and her rational mind-core
(informed by years of Greekish badinage
o'erheard by accident in public baths,
of which, my broken boy, you're virginal,
unwashèd acorn-monkey that you are—
or soon will have been, rather) demonstrates
to her the foolishness of featuring
one whit of anything, nor more nor less
than what her own quintuplitude of sense
presents to her, distrusting even that.
This once was homilized by—what's his name?"

I'm glanced at for a gloss, so say, "D'you mean
that strange philosopher—"

                      "Camp-follower
of Macedonia's bumpkin bully-boy,
who tagged along to Indus, non-shit-pit,
whence come sheer muslins pathics so adore.
Yes, Aceronia, that would be him,
who saw no bush-wool on the gymnosophes,
their funny, skinny, dusky recta free
of buttock muscles' squinching modesty.
They taught him what I'm trying to impart,
and sent him home a somber thinky-Greek.
His name?"

          "Forgot. Ever so copiously
Old Pliny cites his thinkies—or does not.
These 'shrooms are nice with salt, if just a jot."

"Your minister, Graptus, I've also dipped,
like that uncited doubter, and like you,
in sweaty Ganges of Incertitude,
paddling my way to Grade Ipsissimus,
with wrecks and scuttles of this boat called 'me,'
rejections, bondage, deaths, eviscerations,
and—harsher far than these—faith's dire crises,
such as, so subtly, I shall now attempt
inducing in my catechumen, you.

"The Grecians (them, again!) distill black sauce
from colored poppies, efficacious stuff,
medicinal, or magical, or both,
which pathics sip apotropaically
to ameliorate unpleasantness like this.

Your baby sister sucks her candied Chresti
whose ministry is served above the neck
(where you, so far, seem structurally intact).
No lotus dope for me. I navigate
this trepidatious Ocean boatlessly.

   "Semíramis's ardent chums back home,
those Chrestiani she calls 'lions' lunch,'
while waiting backstage at the Colosseum
to have their deathless souls, their torsi, too,
laid open, masticated, same as you,
by teeth, serrated and triangular,
of land dolphins (my joke), will undergo,
quite understandably, tough times like these.
And, in such throes, they dream a secret place
outside the brittle walls of their hometown:
a garden on a hillside, set among
an orchard's olives—"

                "Spado, I would have
that garden rather be an oasis
soft-bubbling in a stand of their date palms,
esteemed worldwide, worth weight in argent coin,
where, like my jar-borne pets, offshoot-Hebrews
in sweetness swim and pray."

                "Or learn to scorn
the sick joke, Aceronia, that is prayer.
I'm teaching laddy-buck useful despair.
To this oasis splinter-Jews repair,
or orchard, in Judea, as you like,
or in their heads, or both, or blent with sand
and gore on the arena floor, there weep,
also perspire blood-droplets, as do, too,

the river horses shipped from Ægypt's mud,
those elephant-sized hogs in scarlet wallows
exhibited at Rome's menageries.
Red sweat's their shed beliefs, the sad entr'acte
of Chrestiani psychodramas, staged
in Bedouin Eleusis, way back east.
(A destination for our touring troupe!)
Ipsissimus, who as 'Father' is hailed,
takes unfaithed cups from non-aspirants' hands,
his will being done, or, vice-versa, theirs un-.
Then follows some stage business with an ear
which Semirámis doesn't care to share.

"Their Kykeon is hemorrhagic hope,
unleavened sops of flatbread, bran-bolted,
from wheat, thrice-winnowed: clearly color-code
for red-white spotty toadstools, such as our—
rather, *your* gr'auntie's sacrament, Graptus.
Jerusalem-ward let us ramble soon
and squirt fun prayer from every hippo pore
and introitus! Who needs bled baggage boys?"

That question prods the poor probationer,
whose postulancy's yet so incomplete.
He's ditched, unneeded, yet's been motivated
in some premortem way I can't quite grasp.

"But, be that as it may, Graptus, much like
those lion-lunches, one comes to suspect—
to know, rather, with certainty—that bare
awareness, puny though it be, is all.
Expiry being but extinguishment
sans residue, no Hades layabout
will loiter, bored, in dull forgetfulness.

No grayness, even: blackness, flat, and silence;
far darker, quieter than any cipher
that you, my servitor, could ever fail
to tally on your porpoise-nibbled digits,
not if your minuscule headhunter's bean
was stuffed with more than one Illyrian's
slight budget of *substantia grisea*.
Pure pitch, quietus, no relief. And numbness.
Must not forget the numbness."

                               Graptus finds,
somewhere, the strength to widen eyes and quake,
as this idea fills, then empties out
his mind the first-last time.

                                  "So terrible!"
he whispers in astonishment.

                                 Spado
insinuates one hand 'twixt self and sand,
unwedging shells from his own under-pudge,
and, with no special rudeness, indicates
"one's cheekies" would feel small disgruntlement
if these last rites were sooner brought to cadence
than later.

                     Dimpled thighs, jostling once more,
produce the selfsame symptoms as before:
The castrate's lap comes suddenly full-gurgle
with brine and dislodged innards.

                                    "You may burp
those facile syllables: 'So terrible.'
But do you *know* it's terrible, Crapped-Us?

Your priestess now exhorts you: take a moment—
though time be short, feeble your servile mind—
and strain yourself to feature this: complete
and utter un-existing. Not what's called
by gymnosophes 'annihilation,' nor
'absorptive union with Unthinking That.'
No bounce-back to the Goddess's embrace.
No boobies, warm and creamy, turquoise-veined.
No merging, none. It's just—"

              "Blackness. Silence."

  "Please let me finish!" our castrato snaps,
belaboring his mother's bargain buy.
A slap or three, no fists, just open-handed
chastisement, light, but in the circumstance
more than effective.

             "Wrong, you smarty-boy!
Not blackness!"

      Slap.

         "Not silence!"

            Slap.

                "Neither,
since each implies the plugging of an inlet,
a sensory organ's failure or cessation.
There's nothing to shut down!"

            Slap.

                              In response,
Graptus's trunk turns loose of something greenish
that, briefly, in a puddle, seems to move.

   "I had an excellent friend," muses the gelding,
abruptly shifting moods, as often do
our nontesticular brethren. Yanking reins
on tempo, she's inclined to reminisce:

   "An un-gauzed pathic. You may recollect
his name. Old Bofus? Frequent visitor?
You probably, my chattel, have forgot,
but when you were a teeny-tiny tot,
some four or five, or eight or nine times, he—"

   "Pyrrho!"

       "Beg pardon?"

                     "Whom you said before.
The name has come to me. Old-timey skeptic,
the tag-along with Alexander, pal
of Indus gymnosophes without the buttocks,
mistrusting evidence of fivefold fungi—
I mean, senses—"

           "Dear lady-in-waiting,
what would we do without you? Anyway,
Old Bofus did not want to live, you see,
and no less often than continually
attempted auto-slaughter, by all means
that suit your more discerning Roman tastes:
impalement on a sword; defenestration
(as indiscreet as that might sound); warm bath

with venesection; aconite commixed
with cinnamon from Felix Araby
in vinous highballs, or administered
by ostrich feather down the gullet jammed,
as in the case of Nero's predecessor,
that mush-mouthed stumble-bum. And, silliest
of all expedients, he'd volunteer
to act pugnaciously in the arena.
And at each crucial juncture, the hard luck
that brought Old Bofus, in the first instance,
to harbor suicidal tendencies,
would cause somebody kindly and/or skilled
to happen by and frustrate him: to splint
his limbs; to tourniquet his veins; to stuff
his guts back in; to induce emesis;
to rim, pre-match, the *retiarius*
whose trident nicked no vitals. Old Bofus,
in fact, was Whoozit Redivivus.

                 "Say,
love-dove, can your attention be unpried
one moment from the bug ambrosia,
to tell the name of that rapscallion
at Troy, the resurrectee?"

                  "Never heard
of him/her. I'm perplexed about this salt.
Salt's what is troubling me. It sparkles, salt,
but alters Chrestus metaphysically."

  "Good point, our better daughter! Carry on.
What was I saying? Oh, yes: Old Bofus.
He's seen what lies beyond, so many times,
and each identical. 'Think *nothing* of it,'

he says, and on that substantive lays stress.
He out-denies even your Momsy-Empress
(who, as you might've noticed, can, at times,
be such a minx, contrary vixen-bitch).
No brash attempt to hawk the heterodox;
no urge to replay Socrates and flout
municipal statutes banning the god-scoff.
It's straight reportage, and precisely why,
until he does, he won't stop trying to die.
A smidgen tuckered out, would be my guess.
He'd envy you, reclining *in extremis*,
so sultrily across my plushy lap.
I, personally, can wait. No rush for me
to leave this beach most plebes call 'human life.'
Aceronia could prob'ly hike or swim.
But as for you, boy, frankly—

      "Oh, hold on!
Do I, perhaps, make you uncomfortable?
Here, let me shift about. Let me raise up
your limewashed sepulchre, then let it down
in matronly solicitude, adjust
your loosened collarbones, this way, then that.
First back, then forth. Again. All better now?
And how d'you like this jaunty angle, here?"

 The Illyrian is nearly killed outright,
not quite, by this custodial display.

 "He was from Elis, in Peloponnese."

 "What? Who? Oh, Pyrrho. Yes, that's nice, sweetie.
You know, stout laddy-buck, I get the sense
you're unenchanted by this dysangel,

this anti-ideation of flat zilch.
Well, with the rule comes one occult exception,
a thing to tote along when skulking off.
I don't suppose you'd like to hear—"

          Graptus
would have lurched forward, if unparalyzed.

"Apparently no need for the hard sell!
Do you recall the longshoreman from Indus,
the one you scrounged at Alexandria
for me to blow that muggy night when starved
for tummy-loads of golliwogster splooge?
That dusky crate-slinger's tradition boasts
a lawgiver, whose name, I think, is Moses.
And Moses says—"

    "Wrong. Manu."

          "Aceronia,
my sad, small snuggle-bunch, you were foetal
upon the floor, as usual, cringing, curled,
throughout the transaction I'm mooting now.
Your ears, apparently, much like your eyes
back there in old Illyria's barber shop,
though buried in your navel, must have worked
right freakishly, for you to've learnt the lore
of that dark Solon better far than I,
who fucked the brute soul-bound to his statutes!
Are we surprised, Graptus? We mustn't be.
'Small jars have large handles,' saith, um—"

          "Ennius,
the pater of our Latin poetry,

who got the soul of Homer from a peacock:
a manly, righteous, staunch Republican
from days when facial congress was frowned on."

"Or grinned around," says Nero's female parent.
"Ignore your prissy sibling, laddy-buck.
The point is that this Indus Ennius says—"

"Not Ennius nor Moses, as I've said,
but Manu, legislator and, in fact,
Deucalion de facto of their race."

"Penníless Enníus, *dux* of Lugdúnum,
your moseying mother's mincing manikin—
who gives a titless trans-Tiberian?
This legal eagle, irrespective of
the moniker that summons him to sessions,
or luncheon, leaves sage words to this effect:

> *Alone what follows beings after death,*
> *when thought, remembrance, motion, sentience, breath,*
> *all trivia to which Heaven entrusts us*
> *are lost, and carcass rots? What else but Justice?*

"Guess what, Grabbed-Ass?"

                                        Our grand Imperatrix
impatiently awaits a prompt reply.

The best our pressed interrogee can do
is, "Wh-h—?"

             "Tardy is how you were today,
and poorly's how you've served the She-God's priest.

Useful Despair

A bad, sad sluggish valet's what you've been.
Guess what will follow you after the D-word.
Guess what, like slow, raw eczema, will eat
into your spirit's tenuous epiderm
for all eternity. Give up? Guess *Justice*.
So, way to go, fuck-tit."

                      I'm looking up
from dealings with a tentative sand crab
whose color I can't fix a term upon,
because I've never touched this fragrant note
or else it's modulating—tough to say.

   A fuddled place inside my stomach's pit
tells me to be appalled, if but a bit,
at something that's been happening next door.
I feel the red and white mycology
consolidate a syllable or so
which, when it comes, comes out like—

                            "Oh, come, come.
Oh, come. He's served you well enough, and long.
Think of the special sweeties he redeemed.
Think of the headhuntress whose pelt he peeled
and tanned with spice of mastiff. With the hem
of your wrecked travel tunic wipe his brow.
Or some such thing."

                    Of all the cryptic glances
the óbese eunuch's shot at me, so far,
most cryptic of them all he's shooting now.
The mindless snail-slime royal retrogress
of Rome's Unconquered Sol's held in abeyance,
as is the Mundus, Known and Un-. All's fixed

upon the sun-sized eyeballs. Both askance,
those orbs, paired Pharos lamps, now flick their beams
on me: an exhortation wordlessly
to gaze into another man's brain-hole,
past individuality's thin rim,
into the crater birthing, gorging all.

   "But, if the end is total," gasps that man,
what is the purpose? Is there not a point?"

   "A purpose? Point?" The Master laughs full out.
"Apart from Moses' 'Justice' con?"

                                "Manu's."

   As cavalrymen who ride ill-tempered mares
soon shed their helmet rivets from the jounce,
so trots our joker on the giggling gut
of a gratified slave owner.

                    "Ha! Good one!
You've done it, Graptus! Chattel makes a funny!
Why could you not have done this once or twice
throughout the life now dragging to full stop,
you wry, sly little bastard? Look! It took
an incarnation's while, but, finally,
climacteric old Momsy's sour puss
upwells with some appreciative snorts!"

   On what appears to be a former shoulder,
the drudge is slugged with joviality.
Another pale, split rib breaches the surface.
This outcome apprehending, the castrato
again slugs, with redoubled heartiness.

"So terrible!" repeats our baggage boy—
or, rather, ex-.

"I frighten you, don't I?
Forget what I just yammered. Block it out.
Distracted, now, let you receive, instead,
the closing benediction of our faith:

She bless thee, she keep thee, she kiss and condole thee.
She shine pretty lovey-face, making thee feel glee.
She slip you her booby, she glut you with boo-hoos.
  She molly, she coddle.
  She golly, she boggle.
She give thee peace freely, and yagga blampf goompee.

"Some barbarous nonsense burps of invocation,"
responds the priestess to my puzzled look,
"quite efficacious at these special times,
as top-shelf Mysteries nowadays confirm."

Our Empress makes a series of mouth-farts.

"It's such a chore to humor spirit-cowards.
Our counsel sessions, Graptus, are suspended
sine die."

"Don't let me—"

"—die a slave."

Ever so softly Spado spoons the mess
into the ebb, which sucks his remnant *exta*
away. Great-Auntie's nephew, with a mouth
awash in alien spume, eyeballs abrading

beneath their lids with foreign sediment,
to tunes of Mistress' tongue trilling a dirge,
expires.

      "Chitterlings and tripe! Sweetbreads and lights!
What would the frowny-faced old haruspex
make of a liver so uncauled in fat?
He'd praise the abstemious proprietress
of such a gland!"

      My fellow runagate
comes rising up on legs like obelisks.
She brushes bushels of crushed crystals wedged
between two pumiced buttocks. She thumbnails
a hundred oyster shells, each countersunk
into the dropsied dimples of her thighs.
De-gritted now, she peers into the body
of land we've somehow to negotiate.

  What towns with colonnaded libraries
might bustle yonder?

        "Now I have no slave
for putting to the torture in my stead
if I should ever go on trial."

          "For what?"

"A potential hostile witness, let's just say,
has been excused from future judications."

"But evidence of drudges under stress
is only heard in cases of incest."

"I have no siblings."

"Yes?"

"No magistrate,
absent firsthand eyewitness tattletale,
could picture any sentient being's submitting
to intimacies with a specimen
like my—excuse me, urp—"

He gags, again,
upon the substantive:

"—mother. My friend,
that is the full extent of what you'll hear
from me, so long's we both, entangled, live,
about that snake-coiffed, tusky-twatted horror."

Utter mortal finality rings forth
from Spado's countertenor, followed up
with two sly, sidelong eyelash bats that say—

"I might just be persuaded."

Curious
or not? For my decision, check back later.
A source of moisture, preferably potable,
is higher on the list of hidden things
that should be wheedled from strange mud today.

Guess whose slim shoulders that chore falls upon.

Books by Tom Bradley

EPIC POEMS

Nagasaki Soul Huffer:
a Manhunt in Fifty-Five Cantos

Injuring Eternity:
a Künstlerroman in Twenty-Six Cantos

Energeticum / Phantasticum:
a Profane Epyllion in Seven Cantos

Useful Despair
as Taught to the Hemorrhaging Slave
of an Obese Eunuch
(illustrated by Nick Patterson)

We'll See Who Seduces Whom:
a Graphic Ekphrasis in Verse
(illustrated by David Aronson)

No Baudelaires in Babylon:
Remarks Presented at the Paris Sorbonne
International Conference
on Electronic Literature

NONFICTION

Put It Down in a Book

Fission Among the Fanatics

New Cross-Fucked Musings on a Manic Reality:
Nonfiction of the Enigmatic Polygeneration

SCREENPLAYS

Three Screenplays

STORY COLLECTIONS

Hemorrhaging Slave of an Obese Eunuch

*A Pleasure Jaunt With One of the Sex Workers
Who Don't Exist in the People's Republic of China*

Calliope's Boy

Even the Dog Won't Touch Me

NOVELS

Elmer Crowley: a Katabasic Nekyia
(illustrated by Nick Patterson and David Aronson)

Family Romance
(illustrated by Nick Patterson)

Felicia's Nose
(with Carol Novack, illustrated by Nick Patterson)

This Wasted Land
(with Marc Vincenz)

The Church of Latter-Day Eugenics
(with Chris Kelso)

Epigonesia
(with Kane X. Faucher)

My Hands Were Clean

Breakfast With Streckfuss

Vital Fluid:
a Hypnovel

Hustling the East:
a Dai Nippon Trilogy

Kara-kun / Flip-kun:
Two Hiroshima Tales

Black Class Cur

Acting Alone:
a novel of nuns, neo-Nazis and NORAD

Bomb Baby

Lemur

The Curved Jewels

Killing Bryce

tombradley.org

www.ingramcontent.com/pod-product-compliance
Lightning Source LLC
Chambersburg PA
CBHW041102070526
44583CB00002B/28